I would like to mention the names of several people who, directly or indirectly, have enabled me to write this book and to whom I am grateful. Firstly, Mr L. Kerssenbrock and Mr Adrian Bloom, who gave me the opportunity. Next, Mr H. G. Hillier, whose large and noted arboretum in Hampshire has been an indispensable and first-hand source of reference. Several members of Hillier's staff, in particular Hatton Gardner, have kindly read through the manuscript and made several useful suggestions, while Desmond Evans provided several excellent drawings. Joan Parsons and June Bartholomew were responsible for the typing, while Susan Lloyd has simply been understanding. Jack Barber, Doug Rugman and the Rev. C. E. Shaw encouraged my interest in plants when a lad. To them I owe my enthusiasm.

Last, but never least, I thank my friend, the photographer Michael Warren, whose patience and skill has placed the rainbow through these pages.

Roy Lancaster

The author and the publisher would also like to express their appreciation in being allowed to take photographs at the following gardens
Bressingham Gardens, Norfolk - (Alan Bloom Esq.)
Earles Mede, Ampfield, Romsey, Hampshire - (D. Earle Esq.)
Exbury Gardens, Hampshire - (Edmund de Rothschild Esq.)
Falkland Palace, Fife - (National Trust for Scotland)
Harlow Carr Gardens, Harrogate, Yorkshire -
 (The Superintendent)
Jermyns Gardens & Arboretum, Romsey, Hampshire -
 (H.G. Hillier Esq.)
Little Park, Flowton, Suffolk (R.A. Brooks Esq.)
Longstock Park Gardens, Stockbridge, Hampshire -
 (The Director)
Green Farm, Mendlesham, Suffolk - (G.S. Pollard Esq.)
Royal Botanic Gardens, Edinburgh - (The Regius Keeper)
Royal Botanic Gardens, Kew - (The Director)
Royal Horticultural Society, Wisley, Surrey - (The Director)
Savill & Valley Gardens, Windsor Great Park -
 (Crown Estate Commissioners)
Sheffield Park, Sussex - (The National Trust)
Talbot Manor, Fincham, Norfolk - (Maurice Mason Esq.)
University Botanic Garden, Cambridge - (The Director)
Westonbirt Arboretum, Gloucestershire - (The Forestry
 Commission)

Overleaf:
Trees both broad-leaved and conifers in a beautiful autumn setting at Sheffield Park, Sussex

TREES

FOR YOUR GARDEN

by Roy Lancaster

FLORAPRINT Ltd, CALVERTON, NOTTINGHAM

ISBN 0 903001 05 5

Roy Lancaster needs little introduction to anyone who is a keen gardener – his name keeps popping up everywhere!
Although this is his first book, Roy is a regular contributor to the popular gardening magazines, writing on a wide range of subjects, and is at present Technical Advisor to the Gardeners Chronicle. *His knowledge of trees and shrubs was gained primarily in the twelve years he has been with Hillier and Sons of Winchester and there can be no better place at which to learn plants. His work there as curator of the extensive Hillier collection and the subsequent publication of their* Manual of Trees and Shrubs *earned him the Royal Horticultural Society's Gold Veitch Memorial Medal, the youngest-ever recipient.*
Roy has travelled on several plant-hunting expeditions, the most notable (and memorable) being a three-month trip to the Himalayas. Through all these achievements (and he is still in his thirties) Roy has remained a very down-to-earth and extremely humorous character, attributes often needed in the many situations in which he has found himself! His enthusiasm is infectious as readers of this book will soon become aware and his knowledge and love for the trees about which he writes is obvious.

The importance of trees

Few of us would deny that of all the plants that we grow in our gardens the tree has perhaps the greatest impact and appeal. Be it for flower, fruit, foliage, habit, or for its shade, the tree forms the kingpin in most landscapes and a focal point in gardens large and small. Whatever the size of a garden and however colourful its flowers, there is something special, almost vital, in having a tree or trees there. Some trees add a new dimension to gardens, that of sound. Who hasn't heard the furious rustling of poplar leaves in a breeze or the rushing sound of a beech canopy in a high wind? Nor must we forget the seasonal activities of trees, particularly those of a deciduous nature. The long cavalcade of buds swelling and bursting, leaves expanding, flowers and fruits developing and so on to the final leaf coloration and fall. Even the movement of different branches in the wind can be interesting.

A tree can be a public attraction, enjoyed by one and all; or, alternatively, a personal, individual pleasure. It is many things to many people. Whenever I see an ancient oak or horse chestnut I think of my boyhood days, and anyone who, as a child, ever climbed into the branches of a large tree will know that detached and independent feeling experienced in sitting aloft, legs dangling, watching the comings and goings of life beneath.

Turning to the practical aspects of a tree, one cannot stress too strongly the necessity of the growing tree to man's health and survival. The trees of parks, gardens and streets are often described as the lungs of a city or town and it is a fact that during daylight hours leaves impart life-giving oxygen to the air while soaking up carbon dioxide. Trees also act as barriers, protecting us from excessive noise, filtering sounds which might disturb or prevent rest, enjoyment or concentration. Trees weaken strong winds, their foliage absorbs dust and their roots consolidate the soil, preventing erosion. The ugliness of many buildings and industrial developments can have as telling an effect on our health and day-to-day living as the noise and fumes of traffic and, here again, trees are playing an increasingly important role in combating this danger.

The economic importance of trees is well known; only the bamboos approach them in variety of usage. However, after hundreds of years of felling and planting for felling, woodlands are once again being allowed, even encouraged, to develop for amenity and recreational purposes. Perhaps, after all, this green and pleasant land will still be fact and not fiction for generations to come.

Finally (though nothing is final in nature), an aspect of the tree not so well known or appreciated is the "micro-life" it supports. Every tree is, in effect, a world of its own. A world populated by birds, beetles, moths, caterpillars, mosses and lichens, to mention a few. The larger and older a tree, the greater and more varied the life it supports; and here it must be stressed that, contrary to popular opinion, not all insects found on or around a tree are necessarily harmful to its good health. As in many other communities it is the harmful minority which claim the limelight.

1

How a tree grows

Without delving too deeply into its life-history, a few simple but essential facts are worth bearing in mind if we are to understand the needs of a tree and therefore its successful cultivation. From a growth point of view, the tree is comprised of four main parts – roots, stem, branches and leaves.

ROOTS

The roots of a tree have two main functions to perform, the first of which is to anchor the tree into the ground. The second function concerns the soaking-up of water and food elements. All roots, particularly the finer (fibrous) roots absorb water from the soil.

The essential food elements (raw materials) required by the tree are carried into the roots dissolved in the water. This partially explains why trees which are transplanted with a good fibrous root system stand the best chance of success. Generally speaking, trees whose root systems have suffered heavy damage establish themselves only with difficulty. Some trees, however, are naturally coarse rooted and rarely produce a close-knit root system. These trees need special care in transplanting and are best planted small.

STEM

The main stem or trunk of a tree has several important functions. First of all, it is a support for the branches, enabling the leaves to be carried up and above the competition from lower-growing vegetation. Secondly, it carries, just beneath its bark, channels (rather like microscopic pipes) along which water and food elements pass between roots and leaves. The main bulk of the stem, certainly the heart wood, is in effect dead (though not rotten) material, serving only to strengthen and support. The bark which covers the stem protects the vital food and water channels from the extremes of cold and heat. Thus it is easy to understand why stripping or otherwise damaging the bark of a tree can lead to serious disorders, permanent injury, or even death.

BRANCHES

The branches of a tree are the aerial extensions of the main stem and are generally arranged in such a way that the leaves have an equal chance to catch the light. Their structure is similar to that of the main stem. Damage to branches may result in their death and, if further neglected, may attract disease, which in turn may threaten the health and possibly the life of the tree itself.

LEAVES

From a utility point of view, the leaves may be regarded as the factories of the tree. Here water, carrying food elements, arrives from the roots and, in the presence of light, energy essential for growth and development is produced and carried away to all parts of the tree's system. During this process, carbon dioxide is consumed by the leaf and oxygen is released into the atmosphere. Through the leaves excess water is released via tiny pores which are mainly situated on the undersurfaces.

If we bear in mind the above facts, it is easy to understand why trees need to be planted where their leaves can catch the maximum amount of light. Few, if any, ornamental trees prefer the shade though some will tolerate it better than others.

While discussing the functional side of a tree, it might be worth mentioning that the flowers are solely concerned with the production of seed. Their varied forms, colours and scents are intended purely for the attraction of insects, but what a happy bonus to the gardener.

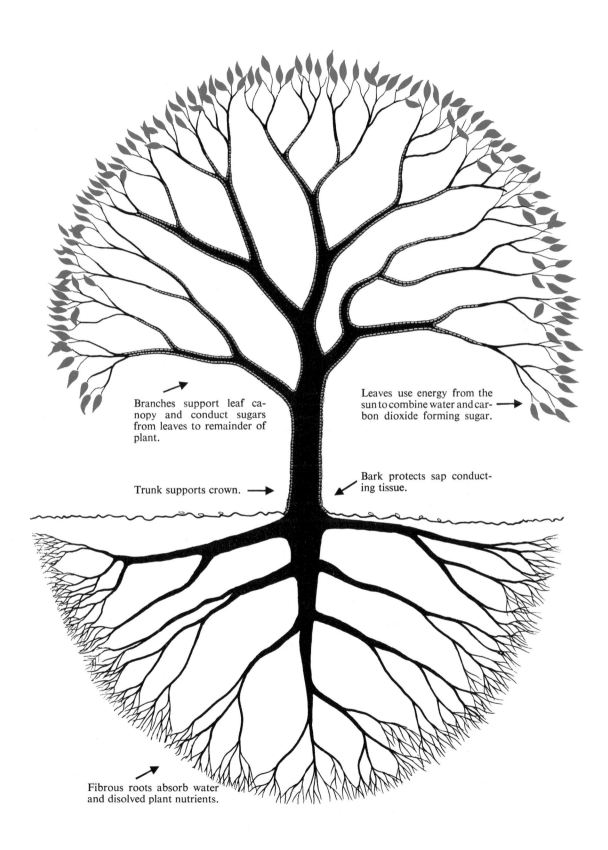

Branches support leaf canopy and conduct sugars from leaves to remainder of plant.

Leaves use energy from the sun to combine water and carbon dioxide forming sugar.

Trunk supports crown. Bark protects sap conducting tissue.

Fibrous roots absorb water and disolved plant nutrients.

Young trees growing-on in the nursery   *Young trees in summer*

How trees are produced

Most people planting trees buy them from a nurseryman. The present chapter, therefore, explains the nurseryman's methods of propagation; relatively simple methods, such as seed and cuttings, are easily practised by the amateur though on a more modest scale.

The nurseryman produces trees by one of several methods depending on the type of tree and its likely sale. Trees which are in great demand need to be produced by the quickest and cheapest means possible. This does not mean, of course, that quality is necessarily sacrificed for quantity; on the contrary, the nurseryman's specialised skills – techniques both old and new – plus the acquired experience, often of several generations, enable him to propagate and to grow a wide range of hardy trees relatively easily.

At the other end of the scale are trees which are difficult to propagate and their production is necessarily a slow, patient and often expensive operation. Of the various methods employed by nurserymen to propagate trees, the following are the ones most generally favoured.

Container-grown young trees

SEED

Seed is the easiest, the most satisfactory, and with some trees, e.g. *Eucalyptus* sp., the only method of propagation. As a general rule, fresh seed give the best results; that is to say, seed should be sown as soon as gathered. This is particularly true of such trees as maples, willows and poplars. Fruits should be gathered when ripe, just as they are ready to fall naturally from the tree. Some fruits, such as the fleshy, berry-like fruits of *Sorbus*, are best netted before ripening commences. This gives some protection against hungry birds.

Large quantities of large seeds, such as oaks, sycamore, chestnuts and beech are best sown in prepared beds, either by broadcasting the seed or, better still, evenly distributing it along shallow drills drawn with the edge of a hoe. A general guide to sowing depths is to sow seed to a depth of approximately three times its own size, i.e. oaks 8–10 cm, beech and sycamore 2 cm, etc. Very fine seed, such as *Eucalyptus*, requires very shallow sowing, i.e. 0·3 cm. When germination occurs, the seedlings may then be thinned-out or, alternatively, left and then transplanted at a later date when further established. Fleshy fruits, such as those of *Davidia*, *Crataegus*, holly and cherry, also ash, are best stratified first. Here the fruits are mixed with moist sand and a little peat (four to one) and placed in a pot, box or some other container, and plunged in a bed of ash or sand outside, preferably at the foot of a north-facing wall. A good tip gleaned from a propagator of long experience is to add to the above mix a little grit scraped from the lane or road. The reason for this is that peat and sand are sterile; therefore by adding road grit one is introducing bacteria which in turn help break down the seed-coat. Germination usually takes place during the second spring though an occasional seed may germinate the first spring or, in the case of holly, sometimes several years later. Seeds of *Sorbus* invariably germinate the first spring.

Trees from seed

When seed of a particular tree is only available in small quantities, and this is normally the case with rare or difficult-to-grow trees, it is best sown in a prepared compost in a pot or other small container. The container should then be placed in a closed frame until germination occurs. Small quantities of large seed such as oak and chestnut may conveniently be sown individually in small pots.

Remembering that some seeds germinate sooner than others, it requires constant and careful checking to spot the first signs of this having taken place. Care must be taken to protect seed sown outside from mice and birds, and the seedlings from snails and slugs. Whether seed is sown in pots, containers or in prepared beds, the resultant seedlings require transplanting and "lining out" at some stage in their development.

Propagators in most up-to-date nurseries now employ other aids, such as chemicals and refrigeration in an effort to assist or quicken germination of certain "difficult" seeds. Various machines are sometimes employed, both for cleaning and sowing seed.

VEGETATIVE PROPAGATION

For a variety of reasons, not all trees produce fruit in cultivation. Some trees which do, produce fruit which develops in the normal way but contains useless (infertile) seed. This state of affairs is particularly common in some species of *Acer* and *Sorbus*, e.g. few specimens of *Acer griseum* in cultivation in England produce good seed. Other trees produce fruits with good (fertile) seed but the resultant seedlings are so variable that only a small proportion in any way resemble the parent. This is often a result of hybridization with other trees of the same genus growing nearby.

Many of the most ornamental trees in cultivation have arisen as seedling or branch "sports" or, alternatively, are seedling forms which have been specially selected for their improved qualities. In the former category are found many ornamental cherries, also trees with variegated or otherwise coloured foliage, such as *Ulmus* × *sarniensis* 'Dicksonii' (yellow) and *Acer negundo* 'Elegans' (variegated); and those of unusual habit, such as *Liriodendron tulipifera* 'Fastigiata' (upright) and

Ulmus glabra 'Camperdownii' (weeping). The second category accounts for some of our finest autumn-colouring trees, such as *Acer rubrum* 'Schlesingeri' and *Quercus coccinea* 'Splendens', also many large-flowered forms, e.g. *Prunus padus* 'Watereri'.

Trees produced as a result of hybridization may or may not produce good seed. Those that do, normally result in seedlings varying greatly in ornamental merit.

Faced with the above facts the nurseryman must resort to other methods than seed to propagate these trees.

CUTTINGS

Many deciduous trees, especially willows and poplars, are still commonly propagated by "hardwood" cuttings taken in winter and arranged in shallow trenches in the open ground. These cuttings normally root in time for planting or "lining out" the following autumn.

An even greater range of trees is propagated by "semi-ripened" cuttings taken in late summer, July–September, when the current year's shoots are reasonably firm and leaves still green. This is certainly the best time to propagate evergreens, such as holly (*Ilex*), *Laurus nobilis*, *Prunus lusitanica* and *Magnolia grandiflora*. Such cuttings are best placed in a closed frame, either inside or outside the greenhouse. The cuttings themselves may be inserted directly into a suitably prepared rooting medium in the frame or first placed in prepared boxes or other suitable containers. The main points to watch are shading (during sunny weather) and spraying. In most nurseries the rooting of "semi-ripened" cuttings is facilitated by the use of special hormone preparations and improved techniques, such as the mist propagation unit. When sufficiently rooted these cuttings are "lined out" in the usual way or containerised.

A third type of cutting is known as the "soft-wood" cutting, taken from the young growth between June and early August according to species. These cuttings may be placed in a frame in the normal way, inside or outside.

Evergreens from cuttings

*Cutting ties on Betula pendula ' Dalecarlica '
35 days after grafting*

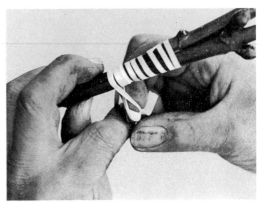

*Grafting Aesculus x carnea ' Briotii ' on to
stocks of Common Horse Chestnut*

GRAFTING

Grafting is the method by which a shoot (scion) of a desirable form is joined by means of a deceptively simple piece of knifework to the stem (stock) of a common type. Successful union will normally only result when stock and scion are of the same or related species. For instance, scions of *Acer rubrum* 'Schlesingeri' may be successfully grafted on to stocks of *A. rubrum*, less successfully on to stocks of *A. pseudoplatanus*, and with no success on to stocks of *A. platanoides*, the latter belonging to a different group. Normally the first method is the most satisfactory.

After cuttings, grafting is the most common method of vegetative propagation practised by the nurseryman. It is also a relatively skilled operation, a craft which is acquired only after a long and patient apprenticeship. It is a method of propagation which comes nearest to the art of the surgeon. An interesting fact which is often forgotten or overlooked is that by this method gardeners were successfully achieving the union of different organs hundreds of years before the first successful human transplant operations.

Grafting is the method by which many of the best forms of ornamental trees are produced in quantity – trees such as *Acer pseudoplatanus* 'Brilliantissimum', *Betula pendula* 'Youngii' and *Robinia pseudoacacia* 'Frisia'. Most coloured and cut-leaved forms of trees, weeping and fastigiate forms, and those specially selected for outstanding autumn colour, as well as slow-growing and difficult-to-grow trees, are generally propagated in this way.

BUDDING

This, in effect, is another form of grafting, usually practised with "easier" subjects, such as ornamental cherries and crabs, as well as many *Sorbus* and *Crataegus* species and hybrids.

LAYERING

This old and popular method of propagation is useful with certain trees which are difficult to root from cuttings. It is generally accomplished by bending a suitable branch down to the ground and wounding a small area by removing a small sliver of wood. The wound may then be dusted with a hormone powder and pegged into the soil. A sandy compost will encourage the formation of roots and a mulch of peat or leaf-mould is beneficial, parparticularly during warm weather. As a general rule, one-year-old branches are the best. After rooting has taken place and the "new plant" is established it may then be separated from the parent plant any time during the following winter.

ROOT CUTTINGS

Certain trees, such as *Ailanthus, Aralia elata, Rhus, Robinia*, etc., may be propagated by preparing, with a sharp knife, 8–13 cm long cuttings of the roots. Best results are more likely from roots taken from young trees (3–5 years) in late winter or early spring. The cuttings may then be laid 3–5 cm deep in a peat and sand (fifty-fifty) compost, preferably in a box. When the cuttings are established they are potted-on and later "lined-out" in the normal manner.

*Grafting :
Stages in development ;
l-r ' Swedish Birch '
(after 35 days) ;
' Snowbell Tree '
(after 18 days)
' Purple Beech '
(after 5 days)*

Choosing a tree

Trees are grown by nurserymen in two ways, either in the open ground or in containers. The former is possibly the older and certainly the more commonly practised method, the trees being lifted from the ground and sold bare-rooted (i.e. roots without soil but with protective cover), or, in the case of large specimens or evergreens, with the roots balled (with soil) and wrapped with hessian.

The advantage of buying trees grown in containers is that they normally suffer little set-back when planted into the open ground. An even greater advantage is that they can be bought and planted at any time of the year, whereas trees grown in the open ground may only be lifted and planted during the winter months. Two disadvantages with container-grown trees is that not all trees prove suited to this method and, as a result, one's choice is often limited. Secondly, although this should not be allowed, many trees left too long in containers become root-bound and establish only with difficulty. This is especially true of fast-growing trees, such as willows and poplars. *Eucalyptus* species are also prone to this trouble and a point worth remembering here is that these trees should be planted as small as possible. A 2 m high *Eucalyptus* looks very tempting in a pot but it isn't the easiest of trees to re-establish in the open ground. Potbound trees are often found to have their roots spiralling to such an extent that it is unlikely they will ever recover and grow normally again. This root insecurity frequently results in the sudden collapse or blowing down of a tree after several years of apparently normal growth. If one buys from a reputable nurseryman or garden centre, however, the troubles outlined above should not occur and trees, by whatever method they are grown, should be of good quality.

Trees as standards; Half-standards and feathered

FORMS OF TREE

Although trees are normally thought of as standards – i.e., with a clear stem and a distinct head of branches – they may also be grown and bought in other shapes, i.e. half-standard, bush and feathered. The standard tree will normally possess a clear stem of approx. 2 m, though some nurserymen can provide trees with stems ranging from 1·5–2·5 m or more. Half-standards normally possess a clear stem of approx. 1–1·5 m. The branch system of both standard and half-standard trees will normally possess a strong straight leader which should develop naturally. Some trees, however, have a naturally dense branch system with no main leader. Several of the smaller ornamental trees such as cherry, crab, thorn, and round-headed trees such as the "Mop-head Acacia", fall into this last group. Trees grown in bush form normally have a clear stem of between 0·3 and 1 m, topped by a branching head. Some of the smaller ornamental cherries, crabs and thorns are sometimes grown this way, while trees such as *Amelanchier lamarckii* are naturally of this form. The "feathered" tree is basically a 1·5–2·5 m central stem with short branches retained to near ground level. Many of the rarer trees, particularly maples of the "snake-bark" group, are usually grown and sold this way. These are usually bought and planted by the customer, who then trains the tree into the required shape by staking the leader and gradually, over several years, shortening and finally removing altogether the lower branches to produce a clear stem. Fastigiate trees such as *Carpinus betulus* 'Fastigiata' and *Populus nigra* 'Italica' are also grown this way, though in suitable circumstances, e.g. in lawns, the branches may be left unpruned to ground level. Several other trees such as common beech, birch and hornbeam are also grown this way when required for "natural plantings".

The form of tree one buys will depend on several factors, including the tree's natural habit, planting site and, of course, personal taste. The main point to bear in mind when choosing your tree, however, is that it should possess a well-balanced branch system. A good fibrous root system is also essential but, as it is rarely practicable to establish this by examination at the time of purchase, one must take it "on spec". Those who, for one reason or another, order "blind" (and the majority of us do), are advised to deal only with reputable nurseries, particularly those recommended by "satisfied" friends or neighbours.

Planting a tree

1. Remove the turf

Generally speaking, trees grown in the open ground may be lifted and planted any time during the period October–late March, avoiding periods of heavy rain, frost and drying winds. Ideally, depending on the season, deciduous trees are best planted from late October to late December when the soil is still relatively warm. Evergreens are best moved or planted during September or October when their roots are most active, although the period April–May is almost as satisfactory. Container-grown trees, of course, can be planted at any time of the year, but the same adverse conditions as mentioned under deciduous trees must be avoided.

WHEN A TREE ARRIVES

As soon as the tree arrives from the nursery, it should be inspected to check that no serious damage has occurred while in transit – young leaders are especially subject to damage in handling. Should the condition of the tree give cause for complaint, this must be made as soon as possible and not left until the cause may prove debatable. If all is ready and conditions are suitable for planting, this should commence. If not, then the tree should be carefully unpacked and "heeled-in", its roots resting in a prepared trench and completely covered with soil. Trees tied in bundles should be unfastened and distributed along the trench. Roots wrapped in sacking may be "heeled-in" thus. Polythene covers should be removed first before "heeling-in". On no account must the roots be left exposed to sun or drying winds. Roots which are found to be dry on arrival should be soaked in water before planting or

"heeling-in". Container-grown trees should be watered as soon as they arrive and, if they are not able to be planted for some time, these too are best plunged in the soil. Trees which arrive during a period of heavy frost, when the ground outside is hard, should be stood in a frost-free shed, garage or outhouse, their roots covered by moist sacking or straw until conditions outside are favourable.

TREES IN LAWNS

The majority of ornamental trees purchased for the garden are planted in lawns. The width and depth of the hole will vary slightly depending on the size of the root system, but it must be large enough to accommodate the roots without the need to bend or break them. A hole 1 m wide and 0·7 m deep should be large enough for the average nursery-grown standard tree. The tree should be planted at its original soil depth (when in the nursery), and this can be checked by noting the mark left by the soil at the base of the main stem.

Having first removed and stacked the turf to one side, the soil should then be excavated to just above the required depth (try the tree in the hole to check this). Having first forked over the floor of the hole, place the turves (grass down) over the broken soil and firm gently underfoot. It is important to provide a newly planted standard or half-standard tree with a strong stake on its windward side to prevent it from blowing over or rocking about in the wind. Sweet chestnut or peeled larch make the best stakes. The stake should be 0·7–1 m longer than the

2. Fork bottom of hole

3. Remove wrapping from roots

4. Prune away damaged roots

5. *Measure tree against stake*

6. *Peat is useful*

7. *Check correct depth of tree in hole*

8. *Gently shake tree to allow soil to perculate through roots*

clear stem of the tree. One end should be pointed and, if possible, the basal 1 m soaked beforehand in a suitable wood preservative (but not tar or creosote). When prepared, the stake should be placed near the centre of the hole and driven into the ground to a depth of approx. 0·3 m. Some of the excavated soil should now be placed back in the hole to form a small central mound. All is now prepared for planting. Trees grown in a container should be placed in the hole and the container carefully removed. Bare-rooted trees should first be inspected to see if any of the larger roots are damaged or broken; those that are must be cut away cleanly with a sharp knife or secateurs. The tree should then be stood in the hole close up to the leeward side of the stake in a position where its stem fits closely to the stake along most, if not all, its length. Mark the stake at a point just below the level of the lowest branch, and cut off its top at the point marked. Having dealt with the stake, the soil is carefully spaced over the roots, shaking the tree gently up and down to allow the soil to filter through the roots, thereby preventing air pockets. This process should be continued until the roots are well covered and then the soil may be firmed gently using the heel of one's boot or shoe, continuing until the hole is filled and the soil is just below ground level. In wet ground the planting may be raised a little above the level of the surrounding area (mound planting). In dry ground the opposite method (basin planting) is sometimes practised to enable water to be applied in quantity should it be required. Either way, the actual soil level must not be allowed to exceed the original planting level (when in the nursery). The tree must now be secured to the stake by means of at least two "tree-ties",

which are specially made for the purpose. Avoid using string, rope, nylon stocking or other temporary and unsuitable ties and on no account employ wire for this purpose. Ideally, one tie should be fixed towards the base of the stem and the other at a point just below the lowermost branch. These will prevent harmful rubbing of the bark against the stake. Finally, the newly planted tree should be given a thorough soaking. This is particularly important with container-grown trees planted during summer.

Young stems are subject to damage from the claws of cats, teeth of rabbits and hares, or even deer. Chicken wire coiled round the tree's base gives protection, but plastic "sheaths" specially designed for the job are now available and are less intrusive. If necessary, peat may be added to the soil during "filling-in" and a "dash" of a suitable granulated slow-acting general fertiliser can be beneficial if added at the same time. If the soil on the site is in any way unsuitable, i.e. very stony, gravelly, dry shallow chalk or heavy clay, it would pay to remove the excavated soil completely and "fill-in" with more suitable topsoil from elsewhere. Trees planted in bare ground may have well-rotted farmyard manure or compost spread in the bottom of the planting hole. The more care and attention given to the planting of a young tree, the better its chances of surviving and flourishing. Many young trees have been lost – and are still being lost – through insufficient preparation of the site, unnecessary and neglected damage to roots and branches, too deep or too shallow planting and bad staking. Always bear in mind that one is dealing with a living thing, like oneself.

9. *A ' dash ' of general fertilizer is beneficial*

10. *Firm with heel of shoe*

11. *Protective ties are essential*

12. *Tree correctly planted*

After-care

It is a sad fact that more young trees are lost through lack of after-care than for any other reason. Many people, having carefully planted and staked a tree then leave it to fend for itself, expecting it to grow from strength to strength without any further attention. The majority of ornamental trees, however, benefit from attention to one or two important details. In fact, I would go as far as to say that, unless one is prepared to take care of a tree after planting, it would be better not to plant it in the first place.

ADEQUATE WATER SUPPLY

The most important requirement of a newly planted tree is an adequate supply of water. Even trees in large areas of bare soil will probably require frequent watering during the first summer after planting. When trees are planted in grassy areas, it is absolutely essential that the circle of soil at the base of the stem (a minimum of 1 m diameter) be maintained for several years, until the tree is obviously well established. Not only does the circle of soil allow easy access of water to the roots it also removes the need for grass cutters to approach too close to the stem. Many serious wounds are caused by attempts to cut grass growing around the base of tree stems. The circle must be kept free of weeds and rubbish, using a shallow hoe or even weeding by hand. To prevent the soil in the circle from drying out during warm sunny periods a 5 cm mulch of grass mowings, peat or leaf mould may be applied, taking care to keep the base of the stem clear. It also pays to check newly planted trees after periods of frost when the roots become loosened and the soil lifted. Simply re-firm the soil with a gentle trampling.

TREE STAKES AND TIES

Once a young tree has become established its stem will increase in girth and, therefore, an annual check must be made to see that the tree-ties are suitably adjusted to allow for the expansion. Many a strong healthy young tree has been throttled by forgotten ties, particularly temporary ties like wire and plastic rope – which, as already stressed, should never be used. Labels with string, cord or wire fasteners are another and similar source of trouble and should be attended to each year. Eventually, when the tree is strong and sturdy enough to stand alone the stake can be removed completely.

Specially made 'Tree Ties' should always be used and checked each year

An unfortunate young tree of the weeping 'Camperdown Elm' in which the stock has been allowed to grow out

Temporary ties are damaging to a tree's development

Bark damaged and suckers developing on neglected Sorbus

1. Branch broken by wind or vandals

2. Cut away top-weight

3. The resultant 'peg'

4. Remove 'peg' flush with main stem

PROTECTION IN EXPOSED AREAS

Trees planted in very exposed sites are obviously more susceptible during the first few seasons than those planted in more sheltered positions. Thus evergreens, and even deciduous trees when "breaking" in the spring, should be given some form of protection against wind. This can easily be done by erecting a simple hessian or polythene screen to the windward side of the tree, or all round the tree if winds come from several directions. This can be dismantled when more settled weather arrives and, in normal circumstances, may be dispensed with altogether when the tree is sufficiently well established to face the blasts alone.

TRAINING AND PRUNING

In most cases a young tree when it leaves the nursery will have the beginnings of its natural shape and habit (see note under "Choosing a tree"). That is to say, if it is naturally tall and straight it should have a definite leader, but if naturally bushy and dense then expect several main shoots. Trees of the former category occasionally develop two leaders and, when this begins to happen, the weaker of the two should immediately be pruned out. A general rule of pruning for ornamental trees is to know the natural shape and habit of the tree and to allow this to develop, as it normally will, only pruning branches which threaten to cross and rub together and those which are damaged or diseased. Trees which have been grafted or budded sometimes throw up suckers from the stock. These should be removed clean from the base as soon as they appear, when they are relatively soft, using a sharp knife. Trees with coloured or variegated foliage sometimes produce a branch which has reverted, producing green leaves. This should be removed in the same way. When about to remove a branch make sure one has adequate and the right tools for the job. A basic collection will include sharp saws, a pruning knife, secateurs and a tin of a suitable wound dressing. For larger trees, a strong ladder and a rope are necessary. In most cases branches are best removed clean from the base, where they join another branch or the trunk. Remove all but the smallest (secateur-size) branches in at least two stages: the first cut 0·7 m or more from the base; the final cut removing the resultant "peg". With large branches it is essential to make an undercut before making the top cut. This will prevent the bark from tearing. After removing any branches the resultant wound should be pared with a sharp knife and then painted with a suitable wound dressing such as "Arbrex".

If the branch is very large or growing in an awkward position, it is wiser to engage the services of a qualified and reliable tree surgeon rather than risk personal injury or damage to property and here I must stress the importance of finding a bona-fide tree surgeon.

Pruning trees, although traditionally a winter operation, is just as satisfactory (if not more so) when carried out in late summer (late July or August). Pruning at this time of the year means that wounds will heal more quickly, while another advantage is that there are less fungal spores floating around thereby reducing the chances of disease infecting the wound. Ornamental *Prunus* should be pruned before mid-July.

5. Pare with sharp knife

6. Wound cleaned and edges smoothed

7. Paint with a suitable wound dressing

8. Wound painted and protected against disease

How trees are named

Trees, like other plants, are given names so that one may refer to them more easily and accurately. Obviously it is much more convenient, when ordering a tree, to give its name rather than have to describe it, and many a wrong tree has been sent because a salesman misinterpreted a rather vague or inaccurate description.

Most people accept that trees should have names; but why, one is often asked, must they be given botanical names, which are difficult to pronounce, complicated and hard to remember? Why can't they be referred to simply by English names?

To understand why, one must first remember that trees are grown all over the world, and when one considers the number of different languages involved, it is obvious that a tree known only by an English name would be regarded with annoyance by a Russian or a Chinese or by any non-English-speaking gardener. Botanical names, therefore, are designed as an international system of naming and all who are interested in trees understand that however many common names a tree may have, it has only one correct botanical name, known wherever that tree may be grown. Mention English holly to an Italian gardener and he probably won't know what you are talking about. Mention its botanical name – *Ilex aquifolium* – and, as likely as not, he *will* understand.

Pronouncing botanical names can be difficult as well as confusing, but it is better to pronounce a name as it reads rather than not at all. Long names can be broken down, e.g. Liquid-ambar sty-ra-ciflua – *Liquidambar styraciflua*.

Although botanical names appear difficult and perhaps "foreign" to the English-speaking gardener, they are well worth learning, telling us, as they do, something about the tree; its country of origin, e.g. *chinensis* – from China; its habitat in the wild, e.g. *sylvatica* – of woods; its habit, e.g. *pendula* – weeping; its leaves, e.g. *latifolia* – broad leaves; its flowers, e.g. *paniculata* – flowers in branched heads; or even the person who introduced it from the wild, e.g. *wilsonii* – after Ernest Wilson. In fact, the usage and meanings of botanical names is a fascinating study in itself and I can do no better than recommend the splendidly readable book: *A Gardener's Dictionary of Plant Names* by A. W. Smith, recently revised by William T. Stearn.

HOW TREES ARE CLASSIFIED

This is yet another fascinating study and basically is again a question of convenience. As far as the gardener need be concerned, plant classification starts at family level.

FAMILIES

These are usually large groups of plants, often including many different-looking members but collectively having several important basic features in common. Family names are always written with a capital initial, e.g. Rosaceae.

GENERA

Most families are made up of smaller groups which, while possessing a "common bond" (shared characteristics), are sufficiently distinct to be separated from one another. The generic name is the first name of any plant and is always written with a capital initial, e.g. *Crataegus, Malus, Prunus*, etc. It may be likened to one's surname, e.g. *Courtney, Thompson, Warren*, etc.

SPECIES

Each genus is made up of from one to many individuals (species), each different in its own way from the next but related to one another by a "common bond". The species name is the second name of any plant and is normally written with a small initial, e.g. Crataegus *monogyna*, Malus *floribunda*, Prunus *sargentii*, etc. It may be likened to one's Christian name, e.g. Courtney *Keith*, Thompson *James*, Warren *Michael*, etc.

VARIETIES

Just as individual people are changeable and have different moods, etc., so species in the wild are variable, often reacting to conditions. These variations (varieties), if permanent, are also given names which, like species, are written with a small initial, e.g. Ulmus angustifolia *cornubiensis*.

CULTIVARS

Garden varieties and specially selected forms from the wild which are maintained in cultivation, are referred to as cultivars. Cultivar names are normally written with a capital initial and enclosed in single quotes, e.g. *Acer negundo* 'Elegans'.

CLONES

The term clone refers to a plant of which all the individuals are identical, having originated from a common source. Clones can only be maintained true by vegetative means (cuttings, grafting, etc.). Most cultivars of trees are clonal in origin, e.g. *Acer rubrum* 'Schlesingeri', *Populus candicans* 'Aurora', etc.

HYBRIDS

Hybrids between two (or more) species are given names which are either the same as a species name but preceded by a multiplication sign, e.g. *Arbutus × andrachnoides*, or simply treated as a cultivar name, e.g. *Prunus* 'Pandora'.

A "FAMILY TREE"
(much simplified)

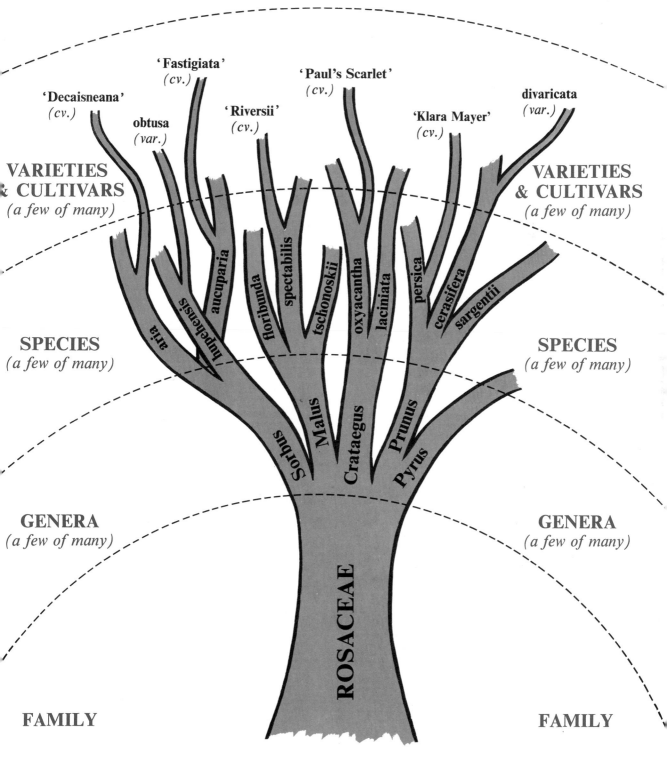

'Decaisneana' (cv.)

'Fastigiata' (cv.)

obtusa (var.)

'Riversii' (cv.)

'Paul's Scarlet' (cv.)

'Klara Mayer' (cv.)

divaricata (var.)

VARIETIES & CULTIVARS (a few of many)

VARIETIES & CULTIVARS (a few of many)

aucuparia

hupehensis

aria

floribunda

spectabilis

tschonoskii

oxyacantha

laciniata

persica

cerasifera

sargentii

SPECIES (a few of many)

SPECIES (a few of many)

Sorbus

Malus

Crataegus

Prunus

Pyrus

GENERA (a few of many)

GENERA (a few of many)

ROSACEAE

FAMILY

FAMILY

13

Pests and diseases

*Aphids
on young shoots*

If one was to list and describe all the pests and diseases which are known to attack trees, the result would read like a "Who's Who" to the Chamber of Horrors. Fortunately, although few trees escape the attentions of certain pests and diseases at some time in their lives, the awful scourges such as the Dutch Elm Disease which threaten to wipe a tree from the landscape are mercifully few and far between.

Perhaps the major curse of ornamental trees is the Honey Fungus, which appears unfussy as to the type of tree it attacks and is a terror in some old plantations where a proportion of the trees are old and weak. Fortunately, it is less common in small gardens unless these are on the site of, or adjacent to, areas of felled woodland.

Fire Blight is another serious disease in certain areas where members of the Rosaceae (*Cotoneaster*, *Sorbus*, etc.) are attacked and often killed. On the pest front, aphids feeding on the young growths can be a nuisance, while scale insects and, in particular, Beech Coccos when present in sufficient numbers can cause serious damage, even to large trees.

Fortunately, a wide range of sprays are available to the modern gardener and as long as expert advice is sought in dealing with these troublesome afflictions, one can readily eliminate or control all but the most serious. Other causes, such as deficiencies in the soil, lime-induced chlorosis, frost damage, sun scorch, etc., can have the appearance of a disease and, therefore, before one can decide on the most suitable treatment, the exact nature of the trouble must first be diagnosed.

Most reputable nurserymen have a member or members of staff whose training or experience has taught them to recognise at least the most commonly met with pests and diseases and general ills. Then there are the various County Agricultural and Horticultural Institutes and Colleges whose staffs can be very helpful in sorting out problems of this nature.

The most important control of pests and diseases, however, is Garden Hygiene, an old-fashioned term which many of today's gardeners don't like because it smacks of time and hard work. As far as trees are concerned, it means keeping them clean of dead, diseased or damaged wood, treating wounds properly, burning diseased twigs and leaves, etc. Thus cared for, your trees will be better able to face trouble, in what ever form it arrives.

USE OF SPRAYS

I would here like to stress the importance of applying sprays, be they insecticides, fungicides, weedkillers, or even fertilisers. Always seek the advice of an expert before choosing anything which might be poisonous to living things other than those you wish to destroy. I suspect that some people throw sprays around as if they were the answer to all evils. Used without thought, care or consideration for possible cause and consequence they are an evil in themselves. Always follow the maker's instructions, particularly with regard to strength and dosage. It is far better to err on the weak side than risk untold damage by increasing the strength. Sprays of any kind should be applied on a mild, overcast and windless day and never on a day when the sun is hot or when a wind is blowing.

In order to prevent the unnecessary destruction of bees and other harmless insects, avoid spraying a tree with insecticide when the tree is in flower. Use the correct equipment for spraying and keep separate the equipment used for insecticides and fungicides and that used for weedkillers.

One final point, or rather, plea. Be sure and store all sprays, whatever their use, in their original containers, securely lidded or corked and locked in a cabinet or cupboard, away from the house and out of sight and reach of children's prying eyes and hands. It could save a life.

Honey Fungus in autumn

A tree for every garden

Such is the diversity of size, shape and effect, that somewhere there exists a tree to suit most, if not all, tastes and situations. There are trees suitable for even the smallest gardens and it should not be necessary to deform a tree by drastic pruning or lopping to make it conform.

Planting a tree which, when mature, will be too large for its position, is all too common these days, nor is it a recent problem. A tour of small gardens on almost any established housing estate will reveal examples of trees planted without any thought for the future.

Foundations weakened or damaged, windows blacked out or completely hidden, pavements obstructed, are just a few of the troubles caused through ignorance of a tree's probable growth and development. Nursery salesmen and arboriculturists, consulted for advice on the choice of a suitable tree, are sometimes assailed with the remark: "I know it will get too big eventually but then it will be someone else's problem." Particularly is this true of many elderly people whose understandable desire for an immediately effective or impressive tree blinds them to their own common sense and the experts' better judgment.

Trouble often arises from planting forest-type trees in relatively confined spaces. Large elms, oaks, beech and lime are fine in parks and large gardens, but when planted in the gardens of the average housing estate they constitute a future headache if not a developing danger.

SOILS

It never fails to surprise me, the number of people who, because they garden on a chalk soil, believe that the choice of trees they may successfully grow is drastically reduced. With few exceptions trees are adaptable to most soils so long as they are not waterlogged. Though certain trees are short-lived or do not give of their best on chalk soils, there are few which actively dislike these conditions. These include such trees as: *Embothrium*; *Halesia*; *Magnolia campbellii mollicomata* and *M.* × *veitchii*; *Nothofagus*; *Nyssa*; *Quercus coccinea*; *Q. palustris* and *Q. rubra*; *Sassafras*; *Stewartia* and *Styrax*.

Trees which are short-lived or otherwise disappointing on chalk soils include *Acer rubrum*; *Amelanchier lamarckii*; *Castanea sativa*; *Eucalyptus* (excepting *E. parvifolia*); *Eucryphia* and *Liquidambar*.

On the other hand, there are some trees which appear to thrive better on chalk soils than on most others. Trees such as *Cercis siliquastrum*, many of the ornamental crabs and many *Prunus*, especially the "Japanese Cherries", certainly appear to flower slightly earlier and with more abandon than their counterparts on, say, clay soils. This is partly due to the fact that chalk soils are basically warmer than clay soils.

ASPECT

The majority of trees described in the following pages prefer an open position, i.e. a position where their leaves receive the maximum amount of light. There are, however, a number of trees which are adaptable, within reason, to shade. These include many of the hollies (*Ilex*); *Gleditsia triacanthos*; *Prunus lusitanica*; *Stewartia* and *Styrax*. The occurrence of shade should not be confused with the provision of shelter, quite another matter. Several "delicate" trees enjoy some form of shelter, usually in the young stage, while some trees which are happy in the comparatively milder areas of the south and west may appreciate the provision of shelter when grown in the north and east and in cold inland areas. Trees which, in the wild state occur in woodland or forest are not normally happy when planted on cold exposed sites. In this category are found *Cercidiphyllum*; *Cornus nuttallii*; *Davidia*; *Eucryphia*; *Nyssa*; *Sassafras*; *Stewartia*, *Styrax*, etc. These trees are happiest when associated with others, though this does not mean to say they cannot be planted as lone specimens in lawns.

TREES FOR EFFECT

I have already mentioned how trees come in many shapes and sizes and are capable of added attractions in the form of flowers, fruits and autumn colour. Some trees also have striped or peeling bark, or coloured twigs which are appealing in winter. One important aspect of a tree, often overlooked, is its foliage value. Many people believe an ornamental tree to be one which flowers. It is well to remember when choosing a tree, that flowers, no matter how colourful, are a temporary feature, and for the rest of the year one is left with leaves and, in the case of deciduous trees, bark and branches in winter. I am not advising against buying trees merely for their floral beauty of course. I feel that it is sometimes worth tolerating a year of possible monotony for the sake of one brief but unforgettable display of flower or, in the case of *Azara microphylla*, a memorable fragrance. But those with small gardens, where there is room for only one tree, quite rightly expect one which will give value for money in the form of several features. Many of these "all-round" trees may be found in the *Sorbus*, *Crataegus*, *Malus* and *Prunus*.

Trees in this book

The trees described in this book, while obviously a personal choice, have been selected with gardens all sizes and situations in mind.   Owners of small gardens will find included a wide choice of suitable and easily available trees, while those with large gardens (now a minority) have not been forgotten and a variety of big trees are also included.   An often forgotten section of the gardening public are those who live in multi-storey blocks of flats. For these people, the planted areas around the base of the building or perhaps the local park, provide their only daily contact with trees.   These council-owned gardens often come to be regarded and referred to by garden-conscious residents as " our garden ", and here perhaps there exists the possibility of " airbound " gardeners suggesting or at least requesting a choice of tree for such areas.   Most forward-thinking councils are only too willing to co-operate with tenants who collectively desire to maintain and improve their surroundings for the benefit of all.   Finally, in an effort to avoid the stereotyped selections of trees described or recommended for planting in many gardening publications, I have included a number of less well-known (to the amateur) trees, most of which match or excel the common sorts in hardiness and ornamental effect.   For this I make no apologies, and though the problem of availability inevitably arises, I firmly believe that the extra trouble some-times experienced in obtaining or establishing these trees is amply rewarded by the challenge and satisfaction of growing something different and new.   Many of our finest ornamental trees are found among conifers and these are dealt with in the companion volume, *Conifers for your Garden* by Adrian Bloom.

EXPLANATION OF SYMBOLS

Size – How fast will it grow? and, How big will it be eventually?, are two of the first things people want to know about a tree they are considering planting. These are, quite naturally, important considerations. However, unlike manufactured articles, trees cannot be made to measure and, due to a variety of reasons, such as soil, aspect, rainfall, etc., trees, even those of the same species, do not always behave in the same way, or grow at the same speed. The following key, therefore, should be taken as indicating the expected eventual size of a tree under average conditions in the British Isles.

> L Large (over 20 m)   S Small (3–10 m)
> M Medium (10–20 m)   VS Very Small (under 3 m)

Habit or Shape – It is difficult, within the confines of this book, to represent the individual habit (branch pattern) of every tree described. The following five basic shapes, therefore, have been selected as being representative and important from a garden or planning point of view.

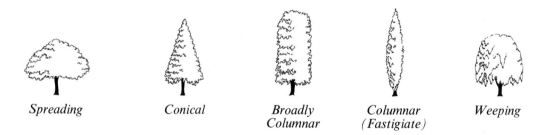

| *Spreading* | *Conical* | *Broadly Columnar* | *Columnar (Fastigiate)* | *Weeping* |

Any deviation from the five shapes is mentioned in the description, e.g.,

Prunus 'Shimidsu Sakura'. A lovely cherry of distinct habit, forming a low, widespreading head of branches, in later life becoming rather flat-topped with the long branches gracefully drooping at the tips.

Award of Garden Merit – Since 1921 the Royal Horticultural Society have shown their regard for excellence in a garden plant by the conference of the Award of Garden Merit (AGM). Many trees have received this accolade, which may be taken as a seal of approval, a recognition of a tree's merit and suitability for general cultivation, eg., *Robinia pseudoacacia* 'Frisia' AGM 1969.

INDEX OF COMMON NAMES

COMMON NAMES	BOTANICAL NAMES	COMMON NAMES	BOTANICAL NAMES
Acacia, False	*Robinia pseudoacacia*	Lime, Golden	*Tilia × europaea* 'Wratislaviensis'
Acacia, Golden	*Robinia pseudoacacia* 'Frisia'	Lime, Silver	*Tilia tomentosa*
Acacia, Mop-head	*Robinia pseudoacacia* 'Inermis'	Lime, Small-leaved	*Tilia cordata*
Alder, Common	*Alnus glutinosa*	Lime, Weeping Silver	*Tilia petiolaris*
Alder, Grey	*Alnus incana*	Maple, Japanese	*Acer japonicum* and *palmatum*
Alder, Italian	*Alnus cordata*	Maple, Norway	*Acer platanoides*
Almond	*Prunus dulcis*	Maple, Paperbark	*Acer griseum*
Angelica Tree	*Aralia elata*	Maple, Red	*Acer rubrum*
Ash, Arizona	*Fraxinus velutina*	Maple, Silver	*Acer saccharinum*
Ash, Claret	*Fraxinus oxycarpa* 'Raywood'	Maple, Snakebark	*Acer davidii; capillipes* and
Ash, Common	*Fraxinus excelsior*		*pensylvanicum*
Ash, Flowering	*Fraxinus ornus*	Maple, Sugar	*Acer saccharum*
Ash, Golden	*Fraxinus excelsior* 'Jaspidea'	May	*Crataegus monogyna* and
Ash, Manna	*Fraxinus ornus*		*oxyacantha*
Ash, Mountain	*Sorbus aucuparia*	Mulberry, Black	*Morus nigra*
Ash, Weeping	*Fraxinus excelsior* 'Pendula'	Mulberry, Weeping	*Morus alba* 'Pendula'
Aspen	*Populus tremula*	Oak, Champion's	*Quercus velutina* 'Rubrifolia'
Aspen, Weeping	*Populus tremula* 'Pendula'	Oak, Chestnut-leaved	*Quercus castaneifolia*
Bay Tree	*Laurus nobilis*	Oak, Cypress	*Quercus robur* 'Fastigiata'
Bay, Sweet	*Magnolia virginiana*	Oak, English	*Quercus robur*
Beech, Common	*Fagus sylvatica*	Oak, Evergreen	*Quercus ilex*
Beech, Fern-leaved	*Fagus sylvatica* 'Asplenifolia'	Oak, Golden	*Quercus robur* 'Concordia'
Beech, Golden	*Fagus sylvatica* 'Zlatia'	Oak, Holm	*Quercus ilex*
Beech, Roblé	*Nothofagus obliqua*	Oak, Hungarian	*Quercus frainetto*
Beech, Purple	*Fagus sylvatica purpurea*	Oak, Lucombe	*Quercus × hispanica*
Beech, Weeping	*Fagus sylvatica* 'Pendula'		'Lucombeana'
Birch, Black	*Betula nigra*	Oak, Red	*Quercus rubra*
Birch, Canoe	*Betula papyrifera*	Oak, Scarlet	*Quercus coccinea*
Birch, Common	*Betula pendula*	Oak, Turkey	*Quercus cerris*
Birch, Himalayan	*Betula utilis*	Oak, Turner's	*Quercus × turneri*
Birch, Paper	*Betula papyrifera*	Ornamental Crab	*Malus*
Birch, River	*Betula nigra*	Pagoda Tree	*Sophora japonica*
Birch, Swedish	*Betula pendula* 'Dalecarlica'	Peach	*Prunus persica*
Birch, Young's Weeping	*Betula pendula* 'Youngii'	Pear, Weeping Willow-leaved	*Pyrus salicifolia* 'Pendula'
Box Elder	*Acer negundo*	Pink Siris	*Albizia julibrissin*
Cherry, Flowering	*Prunus*	Plane, London	*Platanus × hispanica*
Cherry, Autumn	*Prunus subhirtella* 'Autumnalis'	Plane, Oriental	*Platanus orientalis*
Cherry, Wild	*Prunus avium*	Plum, Purple-leaved	*Prunus cerasifera* 'Pissardii'
Chestnut, Horse	*Aesculus hippocastanum*	Pocket Handkerchief Tree	*Davidia involucrata*
Chestnut, Indian Horse	*Aesculus indica*	Poplar, Golden	*Populus* 'Serotina Aurea'
Chestnut, Red Horse	*Aesculus × carnea*	Poplar, Lombardy	*Populus nigra* 'Italica'
Chestnut, Spanish	*Castanea sativa*	Poplar, White	*Populus alba*
Chestnut, Sweet	*Castanea sativa*	Pride of India	*Koelreuteria paniculata*
Chilean Fire Tree	*Embothrium coccineum*	Rowan	*Sorbus aucuparia*
China Tree	*Koelreuteria paniculata*	Silk Tree	*Albizia julibrissin*
Crab, Ornamental	*Malus*	Silver-bell	*Halesia*
Crab, Siberian	*Malus × robusta*	Snowdrop Tree	*Halesia*
Crape Myrtle	*Lagerstroemia indica*	Snow Gum	*Eucalyptus niphophila*
Cucumber Tree	*Magnolia acuminata*	Snowy Mespilus	*Amelanchier lamarckii*
Dove Tree	*Davidia involucrata*	Sorrel Tree	*Oxydendrum arboreum*
Elm, English	*Ulmus procera*	Strawberry Tree	*Arbutus unedo*
Elm, Wych	*Ulmus glabra*	Sumach, Stag's-horn	*Rhus typhina*
Elm, Jersey	*Ulmus × sarniensis*	Sweet Gum	*Liquidambar styraciflua*
Gean	*Prunus avium*	Sycamore	*Acer pseudoplatanus*
Ghost Tree	*Davidia involucrata*	Sycamore, Golden	*Acer pseudoplatanus* 'Worleei'
Golden Chain	*Laburnum*	Sycamore, Purple	*Acer pseudoplatanus purpureum*
Goldenrain Tree	*Koelreuteria paniculata*	Thorn, Cockspur	*Crataegus crus-galli*
Gum Tree	*Eucalyptus*	Thorn, Tansy-leaved	*Crataegus tanacetifolia*
Hawthorn	*Crataegus oxyacantha* and	Tree of Heaven	*Ailanthus altissima*
	monogyna	Tree Privet	*Ligustrum lucidum*
Hazel, Turkish	*Corylus colurna*	Tulip Tree	*Liriodendron tulipifera*
Holly, English	*Ilex aquifolium*	Tupelo	*Nyssa sylvatica*
Holly, Highclere	*Ilex × altaclarensis*	Walnut, Black	*Juglans nigra*
Holly, Yellow-Berried	*Ilex aquifolium* 'Bacciflava'	Whitebeam	*Sorbus aria*
Honey Locust	*Gleditsia triacanthos*	Whitebeam, Himalayan	*Sorbus cuspidata*
Hornbeam	*Carpinus betulus*	Whitebeam, Swedish	*Sorbus intermedia*
Hornbeam, Hop	*Ostrya carpinifolia*	Willow, Corkscrew	*Salix matsudana* 'Tortuosa'
Indian Bean Tree	*Catalpa bignonioides*	Willow, Pekin	*Salix matsudana*
Judas Tree	*Cercis siliquastrum*	Willow, Purple	*Salix purpurea*
Laurel, Bay	*Laurus nobilis*	Willow, Violet	*Salix daphnoides*
Laurel, Portugal	*Prunus lusitanica*	Willow, Weeping	*Salix × chrysocoma*
Lime, Broad-leaved	*Tilia platyphyllos*	Willow, White	*Salix alba*
Lime, Common	*Tilia × europaea*	Wing-nut Tree	*Pterocarya fraxinifolia*

earth would be less fair
without trees,
to grace her valleys,
hide her scars,
cast cool shade
in gardens there.

r.L.

Trees, in autumn, reflected in the lake at Sheffield Park, Sussex.

ACER

This large genus of deciduous trees contains many of the finest for autumn colour, while the "Snakebark Maples" are excellent for small gardens and winter effect. Several of the large species are useful for screening and are tolerant even of industrial situations. All are hardy and, unless otherwise indicated, are unfussy as to soil, though generally thriving on moist but well-drained soils rather than dry ones. Leaves are generally palmately lobed and are arranged oppositely on the twigs. The generally inconspicuous flowers are carried in clusters followed by winged fruits – "spinning jennies".

Acer capillipes

S   **AGM 1969**

Green and silvery-grey striped bark and arching branches bearing 3-lobed leaves which turn orange and red in autumn are the features of this Snakebark Maple. It is a native of Japan and is ideal for a special position.

Acer cappadocicum

M–L

A fast-growing tree with 5- or 7-lobed leaves turning rich butter-yellow in autumn. In the wild it occurs from the Caucasus eastwards to the Himalaya.

Acer cappadocicum 'Aureum'

M–L   **AGM 1969**

One of the best coloured-foliage trees. The leaves are red on emerging, rapidly turning to yellow. Only shows signs of scorch after a long hot summer, otherwise superb and quite happy in an open position. It may be hard pruned (in late summer) to form a large but startling bush.

Acer cappadocicum 'Aureum'.
A 13 year old specimen with branches left to ground level.

Acer davidii 'George Forrest'.
A 13 year old tree showing vigorous arching habit.

Acer davidii

S

Perhaps the best Snakebark Maple for general planting. The green and white striped bark and the vigorously arching branches are best admired in winter. During summer the unlobed, rich green, slender-pointed leaves are borne on rhubarb-red stalks, becoming yellow in autumn. Native to central China where it was originally found by a French missionary – the Abbé David. An excellent form is known as 'George Forrest', who introduced it.

Acer ginnala

VS–S

Sometimes seen as a large bush, this vigorous species from China and Japan develops widespreading branches bearing neatly 3-lobed leaves. These turn to brilliant orange and crimson in autumn.

Acer griseum

S   **AGM 1936**

Few ornamental trees arouse as much interest as the lovely Chinese "Paper-bark Maple". The orange-brown old bark on the trunk and main branches peels prettily to reveal the cinnamon-coloured new bark. In autumn the leaves, composed of three separate leaflets, turn vivid scarlet and flame when the whole tree glows like a bonfire.

Acer japonicum

S

This "Japanese Maple" is often seen as a large multi-stemmed bush although it may be carefully pruned to form a single-stemmed tree if required. It is one of the finest maples for autumn colour when the rounded, shallowly lobed leaves turn from soft green to orange and fiery red. The drooping clusters of small red flowers in spring are also attractive. In common with others of the Japanese Maple group, it dislikes strong winds, draughts and exposure and is best situated in a sheltered or woodland garden, preferably on a moist but well-drained acid soil.

Acer davidii. One of the best of the 'snake-bark' maples.

Acer griseum. A superb small tree with peeling papery bark.

21

Acer japonicum 'Aconitifolium'. *In autumn.*

Acer japonicum 'Aureum'. *Golden summer foliage.*

Acer japonicum
'Aconitifolium'

S   AGM 1957

When happy, this beautiful maple forms a large mound of deeply and sharply lobed leaves which are ruby-red or crimson in autumn.

Acer japonicum
'Aureum'

S   AGM 1969

A very attractive tree, though rather slow-growing. The scalloped, rounded leaves are a bright yellow throughout the year. It is best grown in semi-shade as the leaves are apt to scorch in full sun.

Acer japonicum
'Vitifolium'

S

One of the richest colouring of all Japanese Maples. The large fan-shaped leaves turn a brilliant red in autumn.

Acer lobelii

M–L

The distinct habit of this Italian tree makes it an excellent species for planting in broad avenues and boulevards. It is equally effective of course as a single specimen in the medium-sized to large garden. The upswept branches bear twigs which are covered with a white bloom when young and are clothed with rich green, 5-lobed leaves which turn yellow in autumn.

Acer negundo

M–L

One of the commonest species in cultivation the North American "Box Elder", as its common name suggests, looks nothing like the general run of maples, at least not in leaf. These are pinnate, composed of normally 3–5 separate leaflets. After the willow, poplar and *Eucalyptus*, this is one of the fastest-growing trees and is excellent for screening purposes and rapid effect. In America, sugar is made from the sap. All forms of this tree respond favourably to hard pruning every other year, the resultant strong green shoots bearing large attractive leaves.

Acer japonicum 'Vitifolium'. *A final 'fling'.*

Acer lobelli. A 20 year old tree showing its strong upswept branches.

Acer negundo 'Elegans'.

Acer negundo 'Elegans'

M

The leaves of this effective tree are brightly and irregularly margined with yellow while the young green shoots are covered with a conspicuous white bloom. Unfortunately, both this form and 'Variegatum' are apt to revert and need to be closely watched.

Acer negundo 'Variegatum'

M

This tree is similar to the last except that the leaves are margined white rather than yellow. It originated in France as a sport on a green-leaved tree and was once very popular as a pot plant for foliage effect. One often sees neglected trees which have almost entirely reverted to type.

Acer negundo 'Elegans'. *A young tree with branches hardpruned, encouraging strong shoots and rounded crown.*

Acer pensylvanicum

S

One of the best trees for the small garden, having rather upswept branches with superb snake bark. This is coloured a beautiful pale jade-green with silvery-white striations. The comparatively large 3-lobed leaves turn bright yellow in autumn. It is not one of the best maples for chalk soils.

Acer platanoides

L   **AGM 1969**

A native of Europe (but not the British Isles), the "Norway Maple" is one of the toughest, fastest growing and most popular of the larger species. It is also one of the few maples with attractive flowers. These are yellow and are made more conspicuous in that they appear in bunches from the twigs before the leaves emerge in April. A large tree in full flower really stands out on a cold bleak day. The sharply 5-lobed leaves present an equally colourful display in autumn when they turn to yellow or red.

Acer negundo 'Variegatum'. *A young tree in summer.*

Acer platanoides. 'Spinning Jennies' *in late summer.*

Acer platanoides 'Columnare'

M–L

A distinct form of columnar habit with densely packed branches, becoming a broad pillar of gold in autumn.

Acer platanoides 'Crimson King'

L　　　　　　　　　　**AGM 1969**

This is one of the easiest and most effective trees of its colour with leaves which are crimson-purple in summer.

Acer platanoides 'Drummondii'

M–L　　　　　　　　**AGM 1969**

A strikingly variegated tree in which the leaves possess a broad creamy-white margin. Unfortunately, it is apt to revert and green-leaved shoots must be removed as soon as they appear.

Acer platanoides 'Globosum'

S

In contrast to the tall spires of *A.p.* 'Columnare', this form develops a broad, dense, globular crown. The branches are rather brittle and easily damaged by clumsily placed ladders or climbing children. It presents a ball of yellow in autumn.

Acer platanoides 'Schwedleri'

M–L

Although it will develop into a large tree, this popular maple is perhaps most effective when established specimens are hard pruned every other year (in late summer) to encourage the young growths with their rich crimson-purple leaves.

Acer platanoides. A rich autumn bonus.

Acer platanoides.
The 'Norway Maple' *offers several ornamental features.*

Acer platanoides. Butter yellow autumn leaves

Acer platanoides 'Drummondii'. *Detail of leaves*

Acer platanoides 'Crimson King'.
One of the darkest leaved trees.

Acer platanoides 'Drummondii'. *Striking variegation.*

Acer pseudoplatanus

L

The "Sycamore" is without doubt one of the toughest of all trees, tolerating conditions which would defeat most others. It was the tree most commonly planted by Pennine and Highland farmers to shelter their bleak windswept homesteads. It was also one of the few trees which tolerated the smoke of towns and cities when industrial pollution was at its worst. Although apparently wild in the British Isles it is only native to continental Europe and Western Asia. People with gardens in the country or near parks and woodlands should beware of the grey squirrel, which is partial to sycamore bark and will ruin a tree if not cause its death. Its seedlings, which appear often in great numbers, are best removed the first season, before they become established.

Acer pseudoplatanus. The 'Sycamore' as a specimen tree.

Acer pseudoplatanus ' Brilliantissimum '
Spectacular in spring

Acer pseudoplatanus 'Brilliantissimum'

S   **AGM 1974**

Perhaps the most popular, certainly the most spectacular sycamore, with its glorious shrimp-pink young foliage in spring. Later this changes to yellow-green and finally greenish. It is a highly desirable tree though rather slow-growing. 'Prinz Handjery' is very similar in effect.

Acer pseudoplatanus 'Erectum'

L

A useful sycamore with strongly ascending branches. An ideal tree for city gardens and squares.

Acer pseudoplatanus 'Erectum'. A 10 year old tree showing erect habit.

Acer pseudoplatanus 'Leopoldii'.
One of several variegated sycamores.

Acer pseudoplatanus 'Leopoldii'

L

One of several sycamores with variegated leaves. In this form they are speckled and splashed with yellow and a shade of pink.

Acer pseudoplatanus purpureum

L

The "Purple Sycamore" is so named because of the purple undersides to the leaves. It is very effective when the leaves are blown and ruffled by a strong breeze. A selected form 'Atropurpureum' has leaves darker purple beneath.

Acer pseudoplatanus 'Worleei'

M

The beautiful "Golden Sycamore" has leaves which are yellow during summer. A very attractive tree, particularly when seen from a distance.

Acer rubrum

L

In its native eastern North America the "Red Maple" is considered one of the most spectacular trees in autumn dress. The dark-green 3-5-lobed leaves, bluish-green beneath become rich red or yellow before falling. In early spring the naked branches are bespattered with bright-red flower clusters. In this country it colours best on moister soils, being slow and rarely colouring well on dry or chalky soils.

Acer rubrum 'Scanlon'

M–L

A tall columnar tree which turns into a pillar of red in autumn. A superb tree for smaller gardens and confined spaces.

Acer rubrum 'Schlesingeri'

L

The most reliable "Red Maple" for autumn colour. It is also generally the first to turn, and creates a rich splash of deep red when most other trees are still quite green.

Acer saccharinum

L

A hardy, fast-growing North American tree, the "Silver Maple" is well named as the deeply 5-lobed leaves are silvery white beneath. These turn to butter-yellow or sometimes red in autumn. A large tree is a breathtaking sight when its leaves are ruffled by the wind and the long branches move about. It is, without doubt, one of the most vigorous and attractive of all large maples and ought to be more widely planted in suitable sites. It is commonly planted as a street tree in continental countries. Although it will take normal wind conditions it is not suitable for exposed windswept sites where its branches are subject to damage.

Acer rubrum 'Scanlon'.
A 14 year old specimen of this splendid columnar tree just beginning to 'turn' in early autumn.

Acer rubrum 'Schlesingeri'. A 9 year old specimen in autumn dress. The most reliable form of the 'Red Maple'.

Acer rubrum. Selected clones of the 'Red Maple' colour brilliantly in autumn.

Acer saccharinum 'Laciniatum'

M–L

One of the most graceful trees in cultivation. Its long slender branches are gently drooping, often sweeping the ground and are thickly clothed with deeply and finely cut leaves. 'Wierei' is a specially selected form of even more graceful attributes.

Acer saccharum

M–L

The "Sugar Maple" is one of the most spectacular autumn-colouring trees in North America where, often in the company of "Red Maple" (*A. rubrum*), it illuminates whole valleys and hillsides with its fiery red and orange tints. In the British Isles it is a less spectacular tree, generally slower growing and smaller eventually but still capable of splendid effect in a good autumn when the 5-lobed leaves turn to crimson, orange or gold. It resembles the "Norway Maple" (*A. platanoides*) in general appearance.

Acer saccharinum. A splendid tree in maturity.

Acer saccharinum 'Laciniatum'.
A young tree growing strongly.

Acer saccharum. A 13 year old specimen of the 'Sugar Maple' showing mild autumn tints.

AESCULUS

The "Horse Chestnuts" and "Buckeyes" are among the easiest of deciduous trees to grow, preferring no particular soils or situations. They are a large genus, the majority growing too big for the small garden, and are therefore seen at their best in large gardens, parks and estates. The leaves are generally large and are divided into many finger-like leaflets. The flowers are borne in dense terminal panicles to be replaced by hard brown nuts enclosed in a green, often spiky shell. Autumn colours are normally yellow and can be quite impressive.

Aesculus × carnea

M

After the "Common Horse Chestnut", the "Red Horse Chestnut" is the most frequently planted member of the genus, both as a single specimen and as an avenue. The rose-pink flowers in May are followed by usually smooth-shelled fruits. It is a hybrid between *A. hippocastanum* and *A. pavia*, the "Red Buckeye", although nothing is known of its origin.

Aesculus × carnea 'Briotii'

M

This popular cultivar differs from the type in its generally more compact head of branches and richer-coloured flowers.

Aesculus hippocastanum

L

The "Common Horse Chestnut" is one of the most familiar and commonly planted trees, being particularly popular with children who gather its "sticky-buds" in winter and its fruits – "conkers" – in autumn. Unfortunately, trees in public places are often damaged by sticks and other debris thrown by children in their efforts to dislodge these fruits. Therefore, in such circumstances, the double form 'Baumannii' is to be preferred. The stout, erect "candles" of white, yellow changing to red-eyed flowers in May make this one of the most impressive of all large ornamental trees and, as a consequence, it has long been a favourite as an avenue, village and commemorative tree. Though for so long a part of the English scene, it is native only to the wild borderlands between Albania and Greece.

Aesculus neglecta 'Erythroblastos'. *An 8 year old specimen showing its spring foliage.*

Aesculus hippocastanum

32

Aesculus indica

L   **AGM 1969**

Flowering generally 4–6 weeks later than *A. hippocastanum*, the "Indian Horse Chestnut" is, to some eyes, a more refined tree, with cleaner-cut and therefore more elegant foliage, and longer, more slender panicles of white, pink-flushed flowers. This handsome tree is a native of the north-west Himalaya and is a magnificent tree for large gardens and parks, preferring moist rather than dry soils.

Aesculus neglecta 'Erythroblastos'

M

This slow-growing, uncommon tree reminds one of *Acer pseudoplatanus* 'Brilliantissimum' in that the young foliage in spring is coloured a beautiful shrimp-pink. Later it becomes pale yellow-green, turning to orange and yellow in autumn. It is best planted in semi-shade, sheltered from early-morning sun.

AILANTHUS

Consisting of only a few species these tall deciduous trees are mainly natives of China. They are very fast-growing, hardy and tolerant of most soils and situations, including industrial areas.

Ailanthus altissima. A mature tree of noble proportions.

Ailanthus altissima. Handsome foliage in summer.

Ailanthus altissima

L

Known as the "Tree of Heaven", this handsome species quickly makes a shapely tree, even sending up stout suckers if allowed. The leaves are large and pinnate, composed of numerous leaflets. Male and female flowers are normally borne on separate trees; these are not very ornamental. The bunches of reddish key-like fruits are very handsome on female trees in a good year. This is undoubtedly one of the best trees for planting in cities and towns, as many people living in London will have observed. When hard pruned to ground level, young trees produced strong shoots bearing huge ornamental leaves.

Albizia julibrissin 'Rosea'. *A lovely tree for subtropical effect.*

ALBIZIA

A large genus of deciduous trees and shrubs related to the "Mimosa" and resembling it in leaf. Only two species are in general cultivation, of which the following is the most satisfactory and the one most commonly planted.

Albizia julibrissin

S

Known as the "Silk Tree" or "Pink Siris", this is a small tree with wide-spreading branches, usually becoming flat-topped or umbrella-shaped with age and two to three times as broad as high. The large, deeply divided leaves create a pleasing fern-like effect over which, during summer, hover delightful fluffy clusters of pink-stamened flowers. These are sometimes followed by curious flattened pods. This is one of the best trees for creating a subtropical effect in the garden and is very popular as a foliage plant in exotic summer bedding displays. Although

hardy and able to withstand cold winters, it requires long hot summers to ripen its wood. In the British Isles, it is seen at its best in the south and south-east of England, particularly near the sea, where it is often grown against a sunny sheltered wall. Superb specimens are to be seen on the Continent, particularly in southern and eastern Europe. It is a native of Iran, eastwards to China.

Albizia julibrissin 'Rosea'

S

Similar to the type in habit, this beautiful form differs in the colour of the flower stamens, which are a deep rose, very effective against the fronded foliage. It is hard to imagine anything more satisfying and pleasing than this tree when in full flower.

34

ALNUS

Hardy deciduous trees, the "Alders" are generally grown because of their tolerance of wet conditions, although several have handsome leaves and others long catkins in early spring. They are mainly of vigorous growth.

Alnus cordata

M–L

One of the handsomest species, the "Italian Alder" rapidly makes a tall specimen, its branches clothed with glistening dark-green, heart-shaped leaves, accompanied from summer onwards by attractive cone-shaped fruiting heads. This splendid tree is quite at home on dry as well as wet soils.

Alnus glutinosa

S–M

The "Common Alder" is a familiar native tree of riversides and lakesides, its naked branches strung with yellow male catkins in March. The sticky, stalked buds produce characteristic pear-shaped shining green leaves. It has a wide distribution in the wild from Europe to western Asia and North Africa.

Alnus glutinosa 'Aurea'

S–M

The leaves of this attractive form are bright yellow in spring and early summer, gradually fading to green later. It is more vigorous than *A. incana* 'Aurea'.

Alnus cordata.
A handsome fast-growing tree.

Alnus glutinosa 'Imperialis'.
A young tree of graceful appearance.

Alnus incana 'Aurea'.

Alnus incana 'Pendula'.
An effective but strangely neglected weeping tree.

Alnus glutinosa 'Imperialis'. *Finely cut leaves.*

Alnus glutinosa 'Imperialis'

M
One of the loveliest of all alders. The leaves of this tree are deeply cut into slender lobes giving the tree a delicate and graceful appearance.

Alnus incana

M–L
One of the hardiest and most adaptable of trees, the "Grey Alder" produces hanging male catkins in February and later boldly toothed leaves which are grey-hairy beneath. It is specially useful in cold exposed areas and hails from Europe and the Caucasus.

Alnus incana 'Aurea'

S–M   **AGM 1974**
The young shoots of this alder are reddish yellow, a colour which is maintained throughout winter. The catkins in late winter are orange, while the emerging leaves are bright yellow fading gradually to green in late summer.

Alnus incana 'Pendula'

S
One of the best small weeping trees, the branches forming a dense mound clothed with greyish-green leaves.

AMELANCHIER

A small genus of deciduous trees and shrubs notable for their white flowers in spring and their often rich autumn colours.

Amelanchier lamarckii

S
Sometimes referred to as the "Snowy Mespilus", this easy-to-grow hardy tree creates a cloud of white flowers in spring and says goodbye to summer in a blaze of orange and red in autumn. Usually grown wrongly under the name *A. canadensis* it dislikes dry shallow chalk soils. Its native home is probably North America, although it grows apparently wild in several areas of western Europe, including England.

Amelanchier lamarckii. Rich autumn tints.

Amelanchier lamarckii, flowers in April

ARALIA

Aralia elata. An easy-to-grow small tree valuable for its late flowering.

Only a few species of this useful genus of deciduous trees, shrubs and herbaceous plants are in cultivation, where they are mainly grown for their large, handsomely divided leaves. Though hardy they are best given a site sheltered from strong, cold winds to protect their leaves. They are generally unfussy as to soil.

Aralia elata

VS–S

The Japanese "Angelica Tree" is perhaps one of the best trees for the small garden in spite of its suckering habit. It is easily trained to form a tree and the prickly suckers should then be removed. These make excellent gifts to gardening friends but must be lifted when quite small. The huge Angelica-like leaves, sometimes 1 m long, form ruffs at the ends of the branches and in late summer and early autumn are topped by the large branched heads of white flowers. It makes a bold feature wherever it is planted. A.e. 'Aureovariegata' and A.e. 'Variegata' are attractive variegated forms.

ARBUTUS

A mere handful of species make up this genus of evergreen trees. The three trees here described are tolerant of most soils, even those on chalk. All possess dark-green, leathery, toothed leaves and clusters of small pitcher-shaped flowers. They resent disturbance and so are best purchased as small container-grown specimens. They prefer warm districts and are subject to damage by frosts in cold inland areas.

Arbutus × andrachnoides

S   **AGM 1969**

The superb cinnamon-red peeling bark of this eventually widespreading tree is its chief attraction. The white flowers are produced during late autumn or late winter and are replaced by small red fruits. It is a hybrid between *A. unedo* and *A. andrachne*.

Arbutus unedo

S

The "Strawberry Tree" is usually seen as a rugged picturesque tree with shreddy brown bark. The white flowers are produced during late autumn when the small strawberry-like fruits of the previous year are turning to red. The fruits are edible but insipid. This is an excellent tree for windswept coastal gardens but prefers more shelter in cold inland districts. It is native to the Mediterranean region and south-west Ireland. A.u. "Rubra" is a move compact form with pink-tinged flowers.

Arbutus x andrachnoides. An old specimen showing its impressive peeling bark.

BETULA

The main ornamental attributes of this large genus of hardy, deciduous trees are the rich yellow autumn colours of their leaves and their usually white bark. The "Birches" are mostly elegant trees adaptable to most soils, though growing slowly on those of a dry, shallow, chalky nature.

Betula costata

M–L

A lovely birch from north-eastern Asia with creamy-white often yellow-tinged bark peeling prettily in often large flakes.

Betula ermanii

M–L   **AGM 1969**

A handsome species with creamy-white bark tinted pink, becoming orange-brown and peeling on the branches. It is a native of north-eastern Asia and is sometimes represented in gardens by the variety *subcordata*.

Betula jacquemontii

M   **AGM 1969**

As generally seen in cultivation, this species from the western Himalaya possess perhaps the most beautiful peeling white bark of all the birches. It is well worth seeking out the best forms.

Betula nigra

M–L

Unlike the normal run of birches the "River Birch" from eastern USA is notable for its dark shaggy bark which, with its characteristic diamond-shaped leaves make it one of the most easily recognised species. It is often seen as a picturesque multi-stemmed tree and, as its name suggests, is particularly useful in wet areas, though it will not tolerate permanently waterlogged ground.

Betula costata.
Superb bark especially effective in winter.

Betula costata. A young tree in winter.

Betula pendula. Our native 'Silver Birch' *is a graceful tree.*

Betula pendula. Even in winter there is elegance

Betula nigra. An excellent tree for wet areas, here showing typically dark shaggy bark.

Betula pendula 'Dalecarlica' *with deeply cut leaves.*

Betula utilis. A young tree in the Edinburgh Botanic Garden.

Betula papyrifera. A young tree showing its white bark.

Betula papyrifera

L
The "Canoe Birch" or "Paper Birch" of North America is famous for its striking white outer bark, peeling, often in large sheets, from the trunk. The bark was used for many purposes by the North American Indians.

Betula pendula

M–L　　　　　　　**AGM 1969**
"Lady of the Woods" is just one of the names given to our native "Silver Birch" and aptly describes the grace and beauty of this fast-growing tree. Its white bark and often drooping branchlets make it an ideal subject for lawns, etc., especially when planted in groups.

Betula pendula 'Dalecarlica'

M–L　　　　　　　**AGM 1969**
The "Swedish Birch" develops into a tall slender tree with gracefully drooping branches and deeply cut, long-pointed leaves. It is slender enough to be included in the small garden.

Betula pendula 'Fastigiata'

M–L　　　　　　　**AGM 1969**
A tall birch with closely erect branches. A useful form but lacking the elegance of the type.

42

Betula pendula 'Tristis'

M–L
Another elegant spire-like tree with gracefully drooping branches.

Betula pendula 'Youngii'

S   **AGM 1969**
"Young's Weeping Birch" develops a characteristic broad mushroom-headed habit with branches reaching to the ground. It is an ideal shade tree for the small garden and is the birch version of the "Camperdown Elm".

Betula utilis

M
This birch is regarded as the eastern Himalayan representative of *B. jacquemontii*. The best forms possess a peeling bark of rich orange-brown. I have seen this tree in the mountains of east Nepal, its stems lending warmth to the withered grass and snow.

Betula pendula 'Youngii'.
A young specimen of this elegant weeping tree.

Betula pendula 'Youngii'. A 35 year old tree in an attractive setting.

TREES FOR DIFFERENT SOILS

Chalk Soils	Acer negundo & cvs. Acer platanoides & cvs. Acer pseudoplatanus & cvs. Aesculus (all) Arbutus x andrachnoides Arbutus unedo Betula (most) Carpinus betulus & cvs. Catalpa bignonioides Catalpa x erubescens 'Purpurea' Cercis siliquastrum Cotoneaster (all) Crataegus (all) Davidia involucrata	Fagus sylvatica & cvs. Fraxinus excelsior & cvs. Fraxinus ornus Gleditsia triacanthos Ilex (all) Juglans nigra Koelreuteria paniculata Laburnum (all) Ligustrum lucidum Lirioaendron tulipifera Malus (all) Magnolia grandiflora Magnolia x loebneri 'Leonard Messel'	Paulownia tomentosa Phillyrea latifolia Platanus (all) Populus alba Prunus (Japanese Cherries) Pyrus (all) Quercus (many) Robinia (all) Sophora japonica Sorbus aria Sorbus hybrida Sorbus intermedia Tilia (all) Ulmus (all)
Clay Soils	Acer (all) Aesculus (all) Alnus (all) Betula (all) Carpinus (all) Crataegus (all)	Eucalyptus (all) Fraxinus (all) Ilex (all) Laburnum (all) Malus (all) Populus (all)	Prunus (all) Quercus (all) Salix (all) Sorbus (all) Tilia (all) Ulmus (all)
Damp Soils	Alnus (all) Amelanchier lamarckii Betula nigra Betula pendula & cvs.	Crataegus oxyacantha & cvs. Magnolia virginiana Populus (all)	Pterocarya fraxinifolia Salix (all) Sorbus aucuparia & cvs.

Lakeside trees at Exbury Gardens in Spring.

CARPINUS

Hardy, deciduous trees of which only the following species is commonly planted in cultivation.

Carpinus betulus

M–L
Although most often seen as a hedge, the "Hornbeam" is a splendid tree for planting alone or in groups. Older trees develop a characteristic and attractive grey fluted trunk. The strongly ribbed and toothed leaves turn yellow in autumn while the clusters of peculiar 3-lobed seed bracts hang from the branches. It is a very hardy and adaptable tree of great individual beauty and occurs as a native in east and south-east England (especially Epping Forest) as well as Europe and western Asia, where in the latter region I have seen large forests in the mountains above the Caspian Sea.

Carpinus betulus 'Columnaris'

S
If ever a tree deserved the description "fat" it is this one. Though columnar when young, it soon develops its characteristic egg-shaped habit.

Carpinus betulus 'Fastigiata'

M   **AGM 1969**
A much-planted form which is quite narrow, almost columnar as a young tree but broadening with age.

Carpinus betulus 'Fastigiata'

CASTANEA

A handsome genus of hardy deciduous trees growing happily in most types of soil except shallow chalk soils.

Spanish chestnut.

Castanea sativa, flowering in July.

Castanea sativa

L

The "Sweet" or "Spanish Chestnut" is one of the fastest-growing of all trees and as such makes an excellent screen. The boldly-toothed oblong leaves are accompanied in July by long catkins of pale-yellow flowers which, though individually small, look effective *en masse*. These are followed by the familiar rich-brown edible nuts enclosed in their prickly shells. Trees are variable in their quality of nut and even then require long hot summers to produce worthwhile crops. Old trees develop a gorgeous, deeply grooved, spiralling bark. Although common and apparently wild in parts of the British Isles, it is a native only of southern Europe, North Africa and western Asia.

Castanea sativa. An old specimen showing the characteristic bark.

CATALPA

A small genus of deciduous trees with usually bold foliage and loose terminal heads of fox-glove-like flowers in late summer. They are hardy trees, happy in most soils, but should not be planted in exposed gardens where their leaves with suffer.

Catalpa bignonioides. Flowers in July and August.

Catalpa bignonioides. Slender pods in late summer.

Catalpa bignonioides. A young specimen of the 'Indian Bean Tree'.

Catalpa bignonioides

M   **AGM 1960**

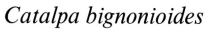

Because of its normally wide spreading habit the "Indian Bean Tree" is only suitable for the medium-sized to large garden and is a favourite park tree. The large heart-shaped leaves, which are late in appearing, are an admirable foil for the white, yellow and purple-marked flowers in July and August. These are replaced after a hot summer by long slender pods. It is native to the eastern USA and is seen at its best in the southern and south-eastern areas of the British Isles.

Catalpa bignonioides 'Aurea'

S–M

A striking form with yellow leaves, one of the best trees of its colour.

Catalpa × erubescens 'Purpurea'

S

A hybrid between *C. bignonioides* and the Chinese *C. ovata*, this tree has the widespreading habit of the former. Its flowers, which appear during the same period, are also similar in colour to *C. bignonioides* but smaller and more numerous. The young shoots and leaves are dark, almost black-purple, maturing to dark green.

47

Catalpa bignonioides. An old tree showing wide-spreading habit.

Catalpa bignonioides ' Aurea '. An 8 year old tree in late summer

Catalpa x erubescens 'Purpurea'. A magnificent specimen in the Cambridge Botanic Garden.

Catalpa x erubescens 'Purpurea'. A young specimen showing strong annual growth.

CERCIDIPHYLLUM

One of the loveliest of deciduous trees, mainly known for its autumn colour, the flowers being insignificant. It thrives best on a moist but well-drained soil, being slow and less satisfactory on dry chalk soils. Cold exposed sites should be avoided as its young growths are subject to frost injury in spring.

Cercidiphyllum japonicum

M

A graceful tree with a single or several main stems and long, slightly pendulous branches. The small heart-shaped bright-green leaves are carried oppositely on the twigs and as autumn treads its colourful path these assume smoky-pink, red or butter-yellow tints when, at the same time, they emit a characteristic aroma of burnt sugar, aparent for some considerable distance. It is native to Japan and China.

Cercidiphyllum japonicum.
A tree of great beauty in autumn. Here seen in the Westonbirt Arboretum.

49

CERCIS

A small genus of deciduous trees easily recognised by their rounded leaves arranged alternately on the shoots and for their small peaflowers which are borne in bunches from the naked branches. Their main requirement is a sunny, well-drained position. They resent disturbance and so should be planted as small as possible.

Cercis siliquastrum

Cercis siliquastrum.
Flowers clustering the branches in May.

S   **AGM 1927**
The "Judas Tree", so legend has it, is the tree on which Judas Iscariot hanged himself. In the garden, however, it is prized for its rose-lilac flowers which inundate the branches in May before the blue-green leaves emerge. In a good (hot) year these are followed by flattened red pods which persist on the boughs into winter. It is native to the eastern Mediterranean region and thrives in full sun. It is excellent on dry chalk soils, and in the environs of Tehran (Iran) is one of the best trees for tolerating extremes of summer drought and winter cold.

Cercis siliquastrum. An old tree somewhere in France.

ORNAMENTAL TREES FOR YOUR GARDEN

Weeping Trees

Alnus incana ' Pendula '
Betula pendula ' Dalecarlica '
Betula pendula ' Tristis '
Betula pendula ' Youngii '
Cotoneaster ' Hybridus Pendulus '
Crataegus monogyna ' Pendula '
Crataegus monogyna ' Pendula Rosea '
Fagus sylvatica ' Pendula '
Fagus sylvatica ' Purpurea Pendula '
Fraxinus excelsior ' Pendula '
Ilex aquifolium ' Argenteomarginata
                                    Pendula '
Ilex aquifolium ' Pendula '
Laburnum alpinum ' Pendulum '
Malus ' Elise Rathke '
Morus alba ' Pendula '

Populus tremula ' Pendula '
Prunus ' Kiku-shidare Sakura '
Prunus persica ' Crimson Cascade '
Prunus persica ' Windle Weeping '
Prunus subhirtella ' Pendula Rosea '
Prunus subhirtella ' Pendula Rubra '
Pyrus salicifolia ' Pendula '
Salix caprea ' Pendula '
Salix x chrysocoma
Salix matsudana ' Pendula '
Salix purpurea ' Pendula '
Sophora japonica ' Pendula '
Tilia petiolaris
Ulmus glabra ' Camperdownii '
Ulmus glabra ' Pendula '

Erect-growing

Acer platanoides ' Columnare '
Acer pseudoplatanus ' Erectum '
Acer rubrum ' Scanlon '
Betula pendula ' Fastigiata '
Carpinus betulus ' Fastigiata '
Carpinus betulus ' Columnaris '
Crataegus monogyna ' Stricta '
Eucryphia x intermedia
Eucryphia milliganii
Eucryphia x nymansensis ' Nymansay '
Fagus sylvatica ' Dawyck '
Ilex (most)
Koelreuteria paniculata ' Fastigiata '
Liriodendron tulipifera ' Fastigiatum '
Malus tschonoskii
Malus ' Van Eseltine '

Populus nigra ' Italica '
Populus nigra ' Plantierensis '
Prunus x hillieri ' Spire '
Prunus ' Pandora '
Prunus ' Amanogawa '
Quercus robur ' Fastigiata '
Salix matsudana ' Tortuosa '
Salix purpurea ' Eugenei '
Sorbus aucuparia ' Fastigiata '
Sorbus x thuringiaca ' Fastigiata '
Ulmus angustifolia ' Cornubiensis '
Ulmus glabra ' Exoniensis '
Ulmus x hollandica ' Dampieri '
Ulmus x hollandica ' Wredei '
Ulmus x sarniensis
Ulmus x sarniensis ' Dicksonii '
Zelkova carpinifolia

Attractive Bark or Twigs

Acer capillipes
Acer davidii
Acer griseum
Acer lobelii (twigs)
Acer negundo ' Elegans ' (twigs)
Acer pensylvanicum
Arbutus x andrachnoides
Betula (all)
Eucalyptus (all)
Fraxinus excelsior ' Jaspidea ' (twigs)
Parrotia persica
Platanus (all)

Prunus serrula
Salix alba ' Chermesina ' (twigs)
Salix alba ' Vitellina ' (twigs)
Salix x chrysocoma (twigs)
Salix daphnoides (twigs)
Sorbus aucuparia ' Beissneri '
Stewartia koreana
Stewartia pseudocamellia
Tilia platyphyllos ' Rubra ' (twigs)
Zelkova carpinifolia
Zelkova serrata

Bold Leaves

Aesculus indica
Ailanthus altissima
Aralia elata
Catalpa (all)
Idesia polycarpa
Juglans nigra
Magnolia acuminata
Magnolia grandiflora
Morus alba ' Pendula '

Paulownia tomentosa
Platanus (all)
Populus lasiocarpa
Pterocarya fraxinifolia
Quercus velutina ' Rubrifolia '
Rhus typhina
Sorbus cuspidata
Styrax obassia

CORNUS

A large genus of deciduous trees and shrubs containing a wide selection of species grown for flower, fruit, foliage or colourful stems. The leaves are normally produced oppositely on the shoots.

Cornus kousa. Star-like flower heads in late may and june.

Cornus controversa.
A 17 year old tree showing tabulated branching.

Cornus controversa

M

A magnificent tree, its branches produced almost in whorls, spreading horizontally to form a distinct tiered arrangement. Its leaves are distinct in being borne alternately on the branches (only one other species of *Cornus* has this arrangement) and turn yellow or purplish red in autumn. The flattened heads of creamy-white flowers crowd the upper sides of the branches in June and July and are followed by blue-black berries. It is a native of China and Japan.

C. controversa 'Variegata'

S

This is perhaps the most beautiful and effective of all hardy variegated trees. Its widespreading branches are produced in tiers and bear comparatively narrow creamy-white variegated leaves. It is slow-growing, but a mature tree is a guaranteed show-stopper.

Cornus kousa

S   **AGM 1969**

One of the most interesting and attractive trees for the small garden, particularly when its spreading branches are covered by the conspicuous white-bracted flowerheads which appear star-like when viewed from above. These appear in late May and June, often followed by strawberry-like fruits which are edible but seedy and insipid. In some gardens the leaves turn to a rich bronze and crimson in autumn. It is native to China, Korea and Japan and relishes a moist but well-drained soil in sun or semi-shade. It cannot be recommended for dry shallow chalk soils.

Cornus nuttallii

S–M

In its native western North America, this is regarded as one of the most beautiful flowering trees. In the British Isles, however, it is comparatively short-lived and never reaches the size of wild trees. It does, however, flower relatively young, and given a sheltered, moist, well-drained position with its head in the sun it will flourish for 15 to 20 years or more. As in *C. kousa* the large bracts are the conspicuous part of the flower-head; these are creamy white, becoming pink tinged and appear quite spectacular in May. Fruits are red as in *C. kousa* and the leaves turn to yellow, occasionally red, in autumn.

Cornus nuttallii.

CORYLUS

Deciduous trees and shrubs of which our native "Hazel" is the most familiar species. All are hardy easy-to-grow subjects for almost any soil.

Corylus colurna

L

The "Turkish Hazel" is normally though rarely encountered in large gardens and parks. Its stately appearance and pale flaking bark make it of interest even in winter, especially when the branches are hung with countless yellow "lambs tails". It is found wild in south-eastern Europe and western Asia.

*Corylus colurna.
A young tree showing
its conical habit.*

SITUATION

Industrial Areas	Acer (most but not A. japonicum) Aesculus (all) Ailanthus altissima Alnus (all) Amelanchier lamarckii Betula (all) Carpinus betulus & cvs. Catalpa bignonioides Catalpa x erubescens ' Purpurea ' Crataegus (all) Davidia involucrata	Eucalyptus (all) Fraxinus (all) Ilex (all) Laburnum (all) Ligustrum lucidum Liriodendron tulipifera Magnolia acuminata Magnolia x loebneri ' Leonard Messel ' Malus (all) Platanus (all) Populus (all)	Prunus (all) Pterocarya fraxinifolia Pyrus (all) Quercus x hispanica 'Lucombeana' Quercus ilex Quercus x turneri Rhus (all) Robinia (all) Salix (all) Sorbus (most) Tilia (all)
Seaside Areas	Arbutus unedo Castanea sativa Crataegus (all) Eucalyptus (all) Fraxinus (all)	Laurus nobilis Phillyrea latifolia Populus alba Populus tremula Quercus cerris	Quercus ilex Quercus robur & cvs. Quercus x turneri Salix (all) Sorbus (all excepting meliosmifolia)
Cold, and Exposed Areas	Acer pseudoplatanus & cvs. Betula (all) Crataegus (all) Fagus sylvatica & cvs. Fraxinus excelsior Laburnum (all)	Populus ' Robusta ' Populus ' Serotina ' Populus tremula Quercus robur Sorbus aria	Sorbus aucuparia Sorbus hybrida Sorbus intermedia Tilia cordata Ulmus (all)

Evergreen Trees	Arbutus x andrachnoides
	Arbutus unedo
	Drimys winteri
	Eucalyptus (all)
	Eucryphia x intermedia
	Eucryphia milliganii
	Eucryphia x nymansensis
	' Nymansay '
		Ilex (all)
		Ilex x altaclarensis
		Ilex aquifolium
		Laurus nobilis
		Ligustrum lucidum
		Magnolia grandiflora
		Nothofagus betuloides
		Phillyrea latifolia
			Prunus lusitanica
			Quercus canariensis (almost
			                evergreen)
			Quercus x hispanica 'Lucombeana'
			        (almost evergreen)
			Quercus ilex
			Quercus x turneri (almost
			                evergreen)

COTONEASTER

A large genus of mainly shrubs but containing several tree-like species which, when young, may easily be trained to a single stem if required. The cotoneasters are hardy, easy-togrow subjects for any soil. All have white flowers normally in May and June.

Cotoneaster frigidus. An excellent small tree trained to a single stem.

Cotoneaster frigidus

S   **AGM 1925**

One of the most satisfactory deciduous trees for small gardens, particularly those in towns and cities, forming a rounded head of branches with comparatively large oval leaves. The heavy bunches of crimson berries weigh down the branches in autumn and remain throughout winter. It is native to the Himalaya.

Cotoneaster 'Hybridus Pendulus'

VS

When grafted on an erect stem this normally evergreen *Cotoneaster*, a hybrid of *C. frigidus*, makes a delightful, if stiffly weeping tree. The hanging branches are crowded with small sealing-wax-red berries from autumn onwards. No garden is too small to contain this tree.

Cotoneaster 'Hybridus Pendulus'. Suitable for the smallest garden, here in autumn fruit.

CRATAEGUS

The "Thorns" are a large, often unwieldy, genus of deciduous, generally small, trees. Being tough, easy to grow and hardy they have often in the past been ignored or relegated to utility jobs such as hedging or for growing where few other trees would survive. Obviously their adaptability makes them of great value in difficult sites, but it should not be forgotten that several species in particular are of great ornamental merit and worth growing for this alone.

Crataegus laciniata. Fruits in autumn.

Crataegus monogyna 'Stricta'. A young tree showing erect habit.

Crataegus crus-galli

S

It is possible that the true "Cockspur Thorn" is no longer in cultivation outside America. However, the tree generally grown as such is a useful subject with thorny branches and glossy, toothed leaves which colour orange and red in autumn. The white flowers in May and June are replaced by red fruits which last well into winter.

Crataegus laciniata

S

The deeply cut, greyish-green hairy leaves of this attractive, slow-growing, Oriental thorn are suitable foil for the white flowers in early June and later for the downy red or yellowish-red fruits. It is an excellent round-headed tree for the small garden, with almost thornless branches.

Crataegus × lavallei

S   **AGM 1925**

This splendid hybrid between *C. stipulacea* and *C. crus-galli* develops a dense head of branches thickly clothed with dark glossy green leaves which are often retained until December. The comparatively large white flowers are replaced by long-persistent, orange-red fruits. It is commonly planted as a street tree.

Crataegus crus-galli. A reliable small tree popular in gardens of all kinds.

Crataegus x lavallei. A dense, small tree with leaves falling late and colourful long-lasting fruits.

Crataegus oxyacantha 'Paul's Scarlet'. *An effective spring display.*

Crataegus monogyna

S

Our native "May", "Hawthorn" or "Quick" needs no introduction. It still forms mile after mile of countryside hedge in spite of short-sighted attempts by many farmers to eradicate it from the English scene. The display of sweet-smelling white flowers in May rivals that of any exotic or foreign tree. It is one of the few trees to withstand both highly alkaline and strongly acid soils, dry or wet, and withstands both industrial pollution and exposure.

Crataegus monogyna 'Pendula'

S

An attractive form with weeping branches and white flowers. A form with pink flowers is 'Pendula Rosea'.

Crataegus monogyna 'Stricta'

S

A useful form of columnar habit ideal for windswept areas and confined places. The flowers are white.

Crataegus tanacetifolia. An unusual but striking hardy thorn.

Crataegus oxyacantha 'Paul's Scarlet'

S   **AGM 1969**

This popular double, red-flowered thorn has been much planted and deservedly so. It originated as a sport of a double pink thorn in a garden in Hertfordshire over a hundred years ago.

Crataegus prunifolia. Colour in autumn.

Crataegus prunifolia. Autumn fruits and tints.

Crataegus prunifolia

S   **AGM 1969**

One of the most commonly planted and most attractive of the thorns. In fact this is a real all-rounder, with a neat rounded crown, healthy glossy-green leaves and white flowers in June. In autumn the leaves ignite in a blaze of orange and red accompanied by bunches of rich red fruits. It is a tree of puzzling origin, most probably a hybrid of *C. crus-galli*.

Crataegus tanacetifolia

S

This unusual and little-planted, slow-growing thorn is perhaps one of the most ornamental. The greyish, hairy, deeply cut leaves are borne on usually thorn-less branches. The comparatively large, white, fragrant flowers in June are replaced by con-spicuous yellow fruits like miniature apples. It is a native of western Asia.

DAVIDIA

The single species which represents this genus is one of the most talked-about and spectacular of all hardy trees. It is hardy and will grow in most soils, though thriving best in a moist but well-drained soil.

Davidia involucrata

M   **AGM 1969**

A vigorous tree with heart-shaped leaves, white-felted beneath, similar in shape to those of a lime tree but more conspicuously veined. In May the fragrant young leaves emerge from the buds accom-panied by small baubles of purple-anthered flowers, each suspended on a slender stalk. These in themselves are of little beauty but are subtended by two large conspicuous white bracts which flutter and shine all along the branches. These bracts have earned for this tree several appropriate common names in-cluding "Dove Tree", "Ghost Tree" and "Pocket Handkerchief Tree". The flower baubles are replaced by hard, green, plum-sized fruits which remain on the branches after the leaves have fallen. This wonderful tree was first discovered by the French mis-sionary, Père David in China in 1869. Al-though fast-growing it does not usually produce flowers until ten years old or more. A variety *vilmoriniana* is commoner in cultiva-tion than the type, from which it differs mainly in its leaves being almost smooth beneath.

Davidia involucrata showing its attractive white bracts

DRIMYS

This small genus of evergreen trees and shrubs contains at least one species which is reasonably hardy in the southern and milder areas of the British Isles. It is a handsome, fast-growing tree, and therefore worth including in these pages for those who seek the unusual.

Drimys winteri

M

The main feature of this species is its bold leaves, which measure up to 20 cm long, pale or dark green above and blue-green beneath. The sweetly scented ivory-white flowers are carried in loose clusters in May, but not on very young trees. Its bark is strongly aromatic and was once used by sailors as a spice to mask bad meat and as a treatment against scurvy. It is native over a wide area of South America.

Drimys winteri. A handsome evergreen for mild areas.

EMBOTHRIUM

Few trees are as striking as the Embothrium in flower. It is a fast-growing tree and requires a moist but well-drained position in full sun to succeed, disliking lime of any kind in the soil. When given shelter of other trees, particularly in woodlands, it tends to become drawn and lanky and may eventually fall over. It also resents disturbance and is therefore best planted small from a container.

Embothrium coccineum

S

In May and early June an established specimen of the "Chilean Fire Tree" may be seen from some distance, its branches thickly crowded with slender-tubed flowers of an intense orange-scarlet or crimson. Hailing from South America it is variable in leaf and also in hardiness. In cultivation those generally sold under the names 'lanceolatum' or 'Norquinco Valley' are the hardiest, and even then are usually most satisfactory only in the south and west of the British Isles.

Embothrium coccineum. Rich flowers of the Fire-Tree.

Eucalyptus dalrympleana. A 17 year old 15 m. tree in the Jermyns Arboretum rocketing skywards.

EUCALYPTUS

The "Eucalypts" or "Gum" trees are a large genus of several hundred species found in the wild almost entirely in Australia where they are as much a part of the landscape as elms were in England. They are fast-growing evergreens with distinctive foliage and often flaky bark and bring a touch of the subtropical to our gardens. Only a comparative few, however, are hardy enough for general cultivation. These are tolerant of most soils but with the exception of E. parvifolia *and possibly* E. dalrympleana *are rarely long-lived on dry shallow chalk soils. They resent disturbance and are normally grown and sold by nurserymen in containers. Small specimens establish easier, and normally make better trees than tall lanky specimens. The leaves of juvenile and adult trees are often very different in shape and size, both being excellent for cutting. The tendency to develop a single tall slender stem may be curbed if so desired by pruning back to near ground level the main stem 1–2 years after planting. This will normally produce a sheaf of attractive sucker growths and a more bushy reduced habit. Flowers of the species here described are white and appear during summer.*

Eucalyptus niphophila. An 11 year old tree. One of the smallest of its kind, the 'Snow Gum' *is suitable for small gardens.*

Eucalyptus coccifera

L

One of the hardiest, the "Tasmanian Snow Gum" possesses a patchwork grey and white bark and clouds of normally silvery-grey adult leaves.

Eucalyptus dalrympleana

L

A most elegant tree, tall and conical as a single-stemmed specimen. The beautiful cream, brown and grey patchwork bark is only marginally more effective than the long scimitar-shaped grey-green adult leaves which are bronze-coloured when young. It is proving very hardy, certainly in the south and west of the British Isles and is reasonably lime-tolerant.

Eucalyptus gunnii

L

The most popular and well-known gum tree in cultivation and hardy in all but the coldest areas of the British Isles. The silvery-blue juvenile foliage gives way to sage-green, sickle-shaped adult foliage, while the flaking bark exhibits shades of grey, cream, green and brown.

Eucalyptus niphophila

S

The "Snow Gum" is perhaps the best species for small gardens, rarely exceeding 10 m and usually seen as a leaning tree of 4–6 m. Its green juvenile leaves give way to handsome scimitar-shaped grey-green leaves, carried on shoots which are attractively coated with a silvery-white bloom. The beautiful grey, green and cream patchwork bark never fails to attract interest and admiration. It promises to be the hardiest of all eucalypts in the British Isles.

Eucalyptus parvifolia

S–M

A hardy gum and one which is tolerant of shallow chalk soils. The small narrow adult leaves are grey-green and the bark grey and smooth.

Eucalyptus gunnii. A striking multi-stemmed specimen in the Royal Botanic Garden, Edinburgh.

Eucalyptus gunnii. A young tree still with much of its juvenile foliage.

Eucalyptus niphophila.
The bark of the 'Snow-Gum' resembles a python's skin.

Eucryphia glutinosa. A beautiful small 'shrubby' tree.
Eucryphia x intermedia. Detail of flowers.

Eucryphia x nymansensis 'Nymansay'.
Flowers in August and September.

EUCRYPHIA

A small genus of beautiful late summer- and autumn-flowering trees thriving best in a moist but well-drained soil sheltered from wind and draughts but open to partial sun. They resent dryness at the roots and should never be planted where the soil is exposed to the sun. With the exception of E. glutinosa *they are tolerant of chalk soils but are rarely seen at their best in these conditions.*

Eucryphia glutinosa

S   **AGM 1935**
Often seen as a large multi-stemmed shrub, this deciduous Chilean species is perhaps the most satisfactory of the genus. Its glossy, dark-green leaves are divided into 3–5 leaflets which turn to orange and red in autumn. The white flowers with yellow stamens resembling small single roses appear in July and August. It is not lime-tolerant.

Eucryphia × intermedia

S
A fast-growing hybrid between *E. glutinosa* and *E. lucida*. The slender branches are densely clothed with ever-green leaves varying from simple to tri-foliolate in shape. These are joined by myriads of small white, yellow-stamened flowers in August and September.

Eucryphia milliganii

VS–S
A delightful species of narrow, erect habit when young, with small neat evergreen leaves and equally miniature white, cup-shaped flowers in late June and July. It is native to Tasmania and is an excellent miniature tree for the small sheltered garden.

Eucryphia × nymansensis 'Nymansay'

S–M   **AGM 1974**
One of the most spectacular trees when in flower. A broad column of dark, evergreen, simple and divided leaves crowded in August and September with pure white, yellow-stamened flowers. It is a hybrid of *E. glutinosa* with the tender *E. cordifolia* and is a feature of many gardens in the south and west of the British Isles.

FAGUS

Although only a small genus, this contains several of the most beautiful, hardy, large, deciduous trees in the northern hemisphere.

Fagus sylvatica

L
No praise is too great for our native "Beech". Both in its dappled green spring attire and its magnificent autumn gold it rivals, if not excels, any foreign tree. Even in winter the huge grey columns of a beech wood demand our attention and admiration. A single, well-shaped, large specimen represents all one could wish for in a parkland or large garden tree. It is tolerant of most soils, reaching perhaps its finest proportions on the chalk hills of southern England. Elsewhere in the British Isles it has been planted and become naturalised. Because of its shallow roots and heavy shade the beech is one of the most difficult trees to underplant. It is distributed in the wild throughout Europe and has given rise to many forms and cultivars.

Fagus sylvatica 'Asplenifolia'

L   **AGM 1969**
The "Fern-leaved Beech" presents a graceful appearance when well grown, its leaves varying in shape from long and narrow to short, and deeply lobed.

Fagus sylvatica 'Dawyck'

L   **AGM 1969**
Slender as a young tree, the "Dawyck Beech" gradually broadens to maturity when it forms an imposing column of green, becoming coppery gold in autumn.

Fagus sylvatica 'Pendula'

M–L
A magnificent tree with high arching and weeping branches, often forming a large dome.

Fagus sylvatica 'Dawyck'. *An 18 year old specimen of the 'Dawyck Beech' in spring.*

Fagus sylvatica 'Pendula'. *Very effective by waterside.*

Fagus sylvatica purpurea. The 'Purple Beech'.

Fagus sylvatica. The grey bark and autumn leaves.

Fagus sylvatica purpurea

L

"Purple Beech". Purple-leaved seedlings often arise in the wild and in cultivation. Several have been given clonal names such as 'Riversii', with deep purple foliage, and 'Cuprea' the "Copper Beech" with paler foliage. All are popular in spite of their "unnatural" colour.

Fagus sylvatica 'Purpurea Pendula'

VS–S

A small mushroom-headed tree with strongly weeping branches and dark-purple leaves. Suitable for the small garden.

Fagus sylvatica 'Zlatia'

M

Sometimes called the "Golden Beech", the leaves in spring are suffused yellow, a colour which reappears in late summer and autumn.

Fagus sylvatica 'Purpurea Pendula'. *For small gardens.*
Fagus sylvatica 'Pendula'. *One of the largest 'weeping' trees.*

Fagus sylvatica 'Zlatia'.
The 'Golden Beech' at its best in late spring.

FRAXINUS

A large genus of tough fast-growing trees with oppositely-arranged pinnate leaves and small flowers of little beauty except in the Ornus *group. They are tolerant of most soils and conditions, including smoke-polluted atmosphere and windswept or coastal areas.*

Fraxinus ornus. The 'Manna Ash' makes an attractive round-headed tree.

Fraxinus excelsior 'Pendula'. *A young tree.*

Fraxinus excelsior 'Jaspidea'

L

Known as the "Golden Ash", the golden twigs of this vigorous tree are most obvious in winter, while in autumn the leaves turn to clear yellow.

Fraxinus excelsior

L

The "Common Ash" is a familiar native tree, easily recognized by its rugged furrowed bark and pinnate leaves in summer and its grey twigs and black buds in winter. The fruits – "keys" – hang in bunches throughout summer and autumn. A valuable timber tree, it is vigorous in both stem and root, being a greedy feeder, and therefore not suitable for small or densely planted gardens. It is tolerant of most soils and conditions, including polluted atmosphere and windswept or coastal areas.

Fraxinus excelsior 'Pendula'

S–M

One of the most commonly encountered weeping trees, its mound-like form being found in many parks and large gardens where it was once planted to form arbours.

Fraxinus ornus

M

Native to southern Europe and western Asia, the "Manna Ash" or "Flowering Ash" has all the good qualities of the common sort with, in addition, attractive panicles of whitish flowers in May. The resultant "keys" are warm brown in autumn. It makes a neat tree with a dense, rounded head. A form of sugar is obtained from the stems.

Fraxinus excelsior 'Jaspidea'. *A magnificent tree at Kew Gardens in autumn.*

Fraxinus excelsior ' Pendula ' - *An excellent mound-forming tree*

Fraxinus oxycarpa 'Raywood'

L

Although relatively narrow and compact as a young tree, the "Claret Ash" opens out in maturity and therefore is not entirely suitable for planting in confined areas. Its leaves are usually borne in threes and the narrow leaflets turn a glorious plum-purple in autumn. Its best colour performances are in full sun or dry or well-drained soils and is one of the few trees which are seen at their best in eastern England.

Fraxinus velutina

S–M

The "Arizona Ash" is one of the best trees for tolerating hot and cold extremes of temperature, as instanced by its success in northern Iran. In drier climates than ours the bark is a striking silvery grey. In the British Isles it is a tree perhaps best suited to the eastern half of England. The young shoots and leaves are covered with a greyish down and the leaves colour butter-yellow in autumn. It is native to south-western USA and Mexico.

Fraxinus velutina. Withstands extremes of temperature. A 16 year old tree.

GLEDITSIA

The most notable feature about this small genus of deciduous trees is the usually formidable armour of the trunk and branches. This takes the form of vicious, large, often branched spines. The leaves are much divided into leaflets, giving them a frond-like appearance, while the insignificant, greenish flowers are succeeded by flattened pods which drape the branches in autumn. They are fast-growing trees tolerant of most soils (except water-logged) and situations, although preferring dry, sunny regions.

Gleditsia triacanthos ' Sunburst '.
Bright yellow young growths

Gleditsia triacanthos

L

The "Honey Locust" is one of the best trees for large gardens and parks in cities, especially where atmospheric pollution is a problem. Its fiercely armed stems, feathery leaves turning yellow in autumn and large pods, often 40 cm or more long, make this a most interesting and desirable tree, particularly in the east of England and in the south of France. It is also shade-tolerant, in which situations the stems are less thorny. It is a native of North America.

Gleditsia triacanthos 'Sunburst'

M

A beautiful form with spineless stems and bright-yellow young foliage throughout the year. It is one of the most effective of its colour.

71

HOHERIA

A small genus of both deciduous and ever-green trees and shrubs from New Zealand. They are best suited to the warmer and milder areas of the British Isles where they are beautiful summer-flowering subjects.

Hoheria sexstylosa

S

Although requiring a sheltering wall in all but the mildest areas of the British Isles, this superb fast-growing ever-green tree is worthy of a place in any garden. Its erect habit and narrow, jaggedly-toothed, glossy-green leaves offset the clouds of white flowers in July and August.

Hoheria sexstylosa. Fast growing and effective when happily placed.

IDESIA

This interesting genus comprises but a single species, a native of Japan and China.

Idesia polycarpa

M

The main consistent feature of this tree is its large, handsome, heart-shaped leaves which are blue-green beneath. The fragrant though insignificant greenish-yellow flowers are followed (in a good year) by large clusters of pea-shaped, green turning to deep-red berries, but only on female trees. Trees of both sexes are required and even then a long hot summer is normally essential to berry formation. It prefers a moist but well-drained soil.

Idesia polycarpa. Handsome foliage

ILEX

The " Hollies " are a large and varied genus, containing both evergreen and deciduous species, many of which in general appearance appear quite unrelated to the familiar " English Holly ". Male and female flowers are generally borne on separate trees and this means that trees of both sexes must be present before berries are produced. In districts where hollies are common there is generally no problem. The hollies here described are popular both as ornamental and utility trees. They are tolerant of a great range of soils and conditions including atmospheric pollution and coastal blasts. The majority develop into tall conical or columnar trees but may be pruned in July or August if growth proves too vigorous. If a formal habit is desired, trees may be clipped (using secateurs) at the same time. Hollies are tolerant of shade but then growth is usually more open and untidy and (on female trees) fruiting less abundant.

Ilex × altaclarensis

S–L
Hybrids between forms of the "English Holly" and the tender *I. perado*, these are comparatively fast-growing evergreens. They are, however, less hardy than cultivars of the "English Holly" in cold northern areas of Europe. Even in Holland these hybrids are subject to frost damage.

Ilex × altaclarensis 'Camelliifolia'

S–M   **AGM 1931**
A superb holly when well grown, its purple young shoots and long glossy-green, almost spineless leaves being enough in themselves to make it a must for the garden. The large red berries therefore come as a pleasant bonus.

Ilex × altaclarensis 'Golden King'

S–M   **AGM 1969**
One of the most effective and reliable variegated hollies. Of strong growth, its leaves are green with a bold yellow margin; they are also smooth or few spined and are effective both alone and when accompanied by the comparatively large red berries.

Ilex × altaclarensis 'Hodginsii'

M–L   **AGM 1969**
This is perhaps the most commonly planted of the hybrids, especially in the north of England where it was and still is favoured for city as well as seaside planting. It is a male cultivar and though no berries are produced its boldly spined leaves are handsomely borne on purple shoots. As the tree matures, the leaves lose much of their armature.

Ilex × altaclarensis 'Lawsoniana'

S–M
A bright and attractive holly, the dark-green leaves marked with a large splash of golden yellow. Unfortunately it tends to throw out green-leaved reversions and these must be pruned out as soon as they appear.

Ilex × altaclarensis 'Silver Sentinel'

S–M
A strong-growing, erect holly of fine proportions clothed with long almost spineless leaves which are green, marbled paler green and grey and boldly margined cream. Berries are produced on older trees. The variegation on young plants, particularly in winter, is more yellow than silver.

Ilex aquifolium

S–M
The "English Holly" is one of the most popular and familiar of all evergreens. As a utility plant it is exceptional, tolerating almost any soil and situation it is possible to find in the British Isles. The red berries borne on female trees during autumn and winter are perhaps the best known of all ornamental fruits, being especially associated with Christmas. It is a native of Europe and North Africa and is commonly orcharded for cutting in parts of North America. There are innumerable cultivars, varying in hardiness, habit, colour and shape of leaf, and colour and abundance of berry.

Ilex x altaclarensis ' Golden King '

Ilex altaclarensis. A tough reliable holly.

Ilex aquifolium 'Madame Briot '. *One of the best of the variegated hollies, with berries as a bonus.*

Ilex aquifolium 'Aurea Medio Picta'. *The Golden Milkboy Holly.*

Ilex aquifolium 'Bacciflava'. *The yellow-berried Holly.*

Ilex aquifolium ' Handsworth New Silver '

Ilex aquifolium 'Argentea Marginata'

M   **AGM 1969**
The common silver-margined holly, normally represented in cultivation by a female clone with attractive berries.

Ilex aquifolium 'Argentea Pendula'

S
Known as "Perry's Weeping", this splendid holly forms a broad mound of weeping branches with silver-margined leaves and abundant berries.

Ilex aquifolium 'Aurea Marginata'

M
This attractive holly is represented by several clones in cultivation, both male and female. All have golden-yellow margined leaves.

Ilex aquifolium 'Aureo Medio Picta'

S
A striking holly in which the green leaves bear a central splash of gold. Both male and female clones are in cultivation and are known either as "Golden Milkboy" or "Golden Milkmaid."

Ilex aquifolium 'Bacciflava'

M
"Yellow-berried Holly". A handsome holly with dark-green spiny leaves and bright-yellow berries.

Ilex aquifolium 'Golden Queen'

S–M   **AGM 1969**
Perhaps the finest of the golden-variegated hollies, with large boldly spined leaves of deep green, marbled and shaded pale green and grey and strongly margined yellow. In spite of its name it produces no berries, being a male clone.

Ilex aquifolium ' Argenteomarginata Pendula '. *A rather splendid high-crowned specimen*

Ilex x altaclarensis 'Lawsoniana'. *A boldly variegated leaf.*

Ilex aquifolium 'Pendula'.
Weeping holly also bears abundant berries.

Ilex aquifolium 'Ovata Aurea'.
A real growing variegated holly.

Ilex aquifolium 'Handsworth New Silver'

S–M　　　　　　　　**AGM 1969**
This is a splendid silver-variegated holly of good habit, with purple shoots, comparatively narrow, white-margined leaves and heavy crops of berries.

Ilex aquifolium 'J. C. van Tol'

M　　　　　　　　**AGM 1969**
This outstanding clone of Dutch origin is, without doubt, the best berrying holly for general cultivation. The leaves are almost spineless and dark glossy green in appearance.

Ilex aquifolium 'Madam Briot'

S–M　　　　　　　　**AGM 1969**
A lovely holly with purple shoots, and strongly spined leaves which are dark green, mottled and shaded yellow and grey and with a golden-yellow margin. In addition it produces large crops of berries.

Ilex aquifolium 'Ovata Aurea'

S
An uncommon but highly desirable holly for the small garden. Of slow growth, it develops a neat compact habit with purple-black twigs and prettily scalloped, spineless, deep-green, gold-margined leaves. It is a male clone and does not produce berries.

Ilex aquifolium 'Pendula'

S
This holly forms a broad mound of weeping stems clothed with dark-green spiny leaves and inundated with red berries.

Ilex aquifolium 'Pyramidalis'

M　　　　　　　　**AGM 1969**
Next to 'J. C. van Tol', this is probably the best holly for berries. These are produced in large quantities, even when other female hollies are having an off-year. The leaves are variable in shape and are often spineless.

JUGLANS

A small genus of deciduous trees, mostly fast-growing, with often large pinnate leaves borne alternately on the shoots. They are unfussy as to soil and situation but are best planted where late spring frosts cannot damage the emerging foliage.

Juglans nigra

L

The "Black Walnut" is a splendid fast-growing tree of noble proportions, with a characteristic deeply furrowed bark and large handsome leaves. It is a native of the USA.

Juglans nigra. A stately tree when mature

KOELREUTERIA

*A small genus of deciduous trees of which the following species is
the one most commonly found in gardens.*

Koelreuteria paniculata

S

Known as "Goldenrain Tree", "China
Tree" or "Pride of India", this beautiful, hardy, widespreading tree is best
suited for the medium to large-sized garden
or park. Its deeply and prettily divided leaves
turn bright yellow in autumn, while the large
terminal panicles of yellow flowers in July
and August are followed by conspicuous
bladder-like fruits. This is a splendid tree,
thriving in a well-drained soil and full sun.
It is a native to China.

Koelreuteria paniculata 'Fastigiata'

S

Ideal for the small garden this form
develops a narrow column of closely
packed branches, decorated with flowers in late summer.

Koelreuteria paniculata. Flowers in July and August

Koelreuteria paniculata.
Excellent for its late flowering. Here seen as a young tree

Koelreuteria paniculata 'Fastigiata'.
Useful where space is limited.

LABURNUM

Only three species comprise this familiar genus of deciduous trees and one shrub. The trifoliolate leaves and hanging chains of scented yellow pea-flowers are easily recognised by most people. The flattened pods contain poisonous seeds and are best removed as soon as flowering finishes. Where young children play it is perhaps wiser not to plant these trees at all. Though comparatively short-lived, they are absolutely reliable in flower and are adaptable to most soils and situations. They are particularly excellent on dry shallow chalk soils.

Laburnum 'Vossii'. One of the most reliable of small flowering trees.

Laburnum alpinum

S

A native of southern and central Europe and cultivated since the late sixteenth century, this is perhaps the most attractive of the "Laburnums", developing a characteristic and picturesque gnarled appearance in maturity. The lush, glossy, deep-green leaves are parted in early June by the conspicuous hanging clusters of yellow flowers. A very small form with stiffly weeping branches is known as 'Pendulum'.

Laburnum 'Vossii'

S   **AGM 1928**

A hybrid between the last mentioned and *L. anagyroides*, this "Golden Chain" is certainly the most spectacular in flower when the long chains of yellow flowers thickly drape the spreading branches in early June. It produces little seed and therefore is preferable to the species for planting in public places.

LAGERSTROEMIA

A large genus of both evergreen and deciduous trees and shrubs, requiring a warm, sunny, well-drained position. The following is the only species in general cultivation.

Lagerstrœmia indica flowering in a town in Southern France.

Lagerstroemia indica

S

The "Crape Myrtle" is a small deciduous tree, sometimes seen as a large shrub, the trunk and main stems displaying a most attractive mottled-grey, pink and cinnamon bark. The small leaves are rather privet-like in appearance and often colour effectively in late autumn. The beautiful, crinkly-petalled flowers are borne in panicles at the ends of the current year's shoots, and though formed in summer, do not open until late summer and autumn. In colour they vary from lilac-pink to red or even white, a well-shaped tree in full flower presenting a magnificent sight. This superb flowering tree is a feature of many continental cities and towns, particularly in southern and eastern Europe. In order to flower well, it requires a long, continuously hot summer and, in the British Isles, is perhaps only worth considering in southern and south-eastern regions of England, even here, against a sunny, sheltered wall. It is a native of China and Korea.

LAURUS

This genus comprises only two species of evergreen trees, of which only one is at all well known.

Laurus nobilis

S

The "Bay Laurel" is an excellent evergreen, particularly when used in formal surroundings. Its leathery, spicily aromatic leaves are well known to the housewife and cook. Less familiar are the shining black, cherry-like fruits borne on female trees during summer. It was the leafy sprigs of this tree which formed the victor's crown of the Greeks and Romans. It is a native of the Mediterranean region and will grow in most soils but is subject to winter damage in cold inland areas.

Laurus nobilis 'Aurea'

S

A striking form with golden-yellow leaves, particularly effective during winter and spring when it gives a welcome splash of bright colour.

Laurus nobilis. The 'Bay' is attractive when in flower.

"TREES FOR SMALL GARDENS"

Acer capillipes
Acer davidii
Acer ginnala
Acer griseum
Acer japonicum
Acer pensylvanicum
Acer pseudoplatanus 'Brilliantissimum'
Alnus incana 'Pendula'
Amelanchier lamarckii
Aralia elata
Betula pendula 'Youngii'
Carpinus betulus 'Columnaris'
Cercis siliquastrum
Cornus
Cornus kousa
Cornus nuttallii
Cotoneaster frigidus
Cotoneaster 'Hybridus Pendulus'
Cotoneaster x watereri
Crataegus (most)
Embothrium coccineum
Eucalyptus niphophila

Eucryphia glutinosa
Eucryphia x intermedia
Eucryphia milliganii
Fagus sylvatica 'Purpurea Pendula'
Hoheria sexstylosa
Ilex aquifolium 'Argentea Pendula'
Ilex aquifolium 'Aureo Medio Picta'
Ilex aquifolium 'Ovata Aurea'
Ilex aquifolium 'Pendula'
Koelreuteria paniculata 'Fastigiata'
Laburnum alpinum
Laburnum 'Vossii'
Laurus nobilis
Magnolia grandiflora
Magnolia x loebneri 'Leonard Messel'
Magnolia virginiana
Malus (many)
Morus alba 'Pendula'
Morus nigra
Phillyrea latifolia
Populus tremula 'Pendula'

Prunus (many)
Pyrus nivalis
Pyrus salicifolia 'Pendula'
Quercus robur 'Concordia'
Rhus trichocarpa
Rhus typhina
Robinia x hillieri
Robinia pseudoacacia 'Frisia'
Robinia pseudoacacia 'Inermis'
Robinia pseudoacacia 'Rozynskyana'
Salix aegyptiaca
Salix caprea 'Pendula'
Salix daphnoides
Salix purpurea
Sophora japonica 'Pendula'
Sorbus (most)
Stewartia koreana
Stewartia pseudocamellia
Styrax japonica
Styrax obassia
Tilia mongolica

LIGUSTRUM

The privets are a small but variable group of trees and shrubs tolerant of most soils and situations. Many people think only of the hedging "Privet" (L. ovalifolium) when the name arises, which is a pity, as there are several first-class species well worth growing for flowers and fruit.

Ligustrum lucidum

S–M

The "Tree Privet" is a superb ever-green tree from China, suitable for a special position. The comparatively large, glossy, dark-green, leathery leaves are borne in a dense, rounded head which, in autumn, is transformed by the panicles of creamy-white flowers which terminate the shoots into a striking display noticeable from a considerable distance. Large speci-mens develop an attractive grey fluted trunk.

Ligustrum lucidum 'Excelsum Superbum'

S

A striking form in which the leaves are mottled and margined creamy white and yellow. It is less hardy than the type and is best planted where cold blasts cannot singe the young spring growths.

Ligustrum lucidum. A handsome 'Tree Privet'. Useful also for its late flowering.

LIQUIDAMBAR

A small genus of deciduous trees with usually 5-lobed leaves colouring richly in autumn. The flowers are insignificant. They thrive best in a moist but well-drained soil and are not suitable for dry shallow chalk soils.

Liquidambar styraciflua

L   **AGM 1969**

One of the finest trees in autumn when the handsomely lobed leaves turn to shades of crimson or purple. It is occasionally mistaken for a maple (*Acer* sp.) but the alternately arranged leaves easily distinguish it. It is a native of the eastern USA where it is known as the "Sweet Gum".

Liquidambar styraciflua. The best forms colour richly in autumn.

Liquidambar styraciflua. A young tree turning in autumn. Here the lower branches have been retained.

Liquidambar styraciflua. A young tree in summer.

LIRIODENDRON

Only two species of deciduous trees represent this interesting genus. Both are hardy and fast-growing, happy in most soils, including those on chalk, but thriving best in a deep, moist, well-drained loam. The leaves of these trees are like no others in cultivation.

Liriodendron tulipifera

L
The "Tulip Tree" is, without doubt, one of the finest ornamental trees in the temperate regions. It is one of the select band of trees to which the description stately can be applied. Its peculiar 4-lobed, saddle-shaped leaves are attractive at all times, especially in autumn when they turn to butter-yellow. The common name for this tree refers to the cup-shaped flowers which are yellowish green in colour, marked orange within. These are produced at the ends of the branches in June and July, but not on young trees. It is a native of eastern North America.

Liriodendron tulipifera 'Aureomarginatum'

L
A striking form in which the leaves possess a broad border of yellow, brighter in spring and becoming yellowish green in late summer.

Liriodendron tulipifera 'Fastigiatum'

M
A comparatively fast-growing tree, narrow when young, broadening with age. It is particularly suited for medium-sized gardens and is especially effective in autumn when it stands like a pillar of gold.

Liriodendron tulipifera.
A young specimen not yet flowered.

Liriodendron tulipifera. A noble tree in early autumn

84

Liriodendron tulipifera ' Aureomarginatum '. *Pleasantly effective variegation*

Liriodendron tulipifera 'Fastigiatum'.
A 12 year old specimen.

Liriodendron tulipifera.
Tulip - shaped flowers in summer.

MAGNOLIA

A "Magnolia" is what many people picture when they talk of an exotic flower, and it is true that there are few hardy trees with flowers so large and so breathtaking. They are a variable crowd, ranging from shrubs to trees, both deciduous and evergreen. On some species flowers are borne in late winter or early spring before the leaves, while others flower among the leaves in summer. Though tolerant of heavy clay soils and atmospheric pollution, they thrive best in a moist but well-drained soil. Only a few are successful on shallow chalk soils.

Magnolia virginiana. The Sweet Bay produces its fragrant flowers over a long period.

Magnolia grandiflora. Flowers throughout summer

Magnolia acuminata

L

Known as the "Cucumber Tree", in reference to its young fruits, this fast-growing species from the eastern USA is mainly valued for its handsome large foliage. The comparatively small, dull, greenish-yellow flowers are produced with the leaves during May and June.

Magnolia grandiflora

S

Only two evergreen magnolias are grown in general cultivation and this species is the more well known and certainly the most satisfactory. It is usually seen against a warm sheltering wall and requires this in colder areas; however, in warmer localities it makes an imposing freestanding specimen. Old specimens are often gnarled and full of character. The large, bright-green leathery leaves are shining above and clothed with rust-coloured hairs beneath at least when young. The large, fragrant, creamy-white, globular flowers appear at the ends of the shoots during late summer and early autumn. It is fairly tolerant of chalk soils and is a native of the south-eastern USA. There are several selected named clones, which, due to being grafted, have the advantage of flowering at an earlier age than those grown from seed.

Magnolia × loebneri 'Leonard Messel'

S

This award-winning magnolia is a hybrid between the shrubby *M. stellata* 'Rosea' and the tree *M. kobus*, combining several good garden qualities. First of all it is hardy and secondly it grows quite well on chalk soils. Its star-shaped flowers, which are produced even on small specimens, are lilac-pink, darker in bud and decorate the slender branches before the leaves in April.

Magnolia x loebneri 'Leonard Messel'.
Pink in bud paling with age. A 5 year old
specimen flowering when quite young.

Magnolia x soulangiana.
Magnolia acuminata.
An 11 year old tree showing handsome foliage

Magnolia x soulangiana

S   A.G.M. 1932

A hybrid between *Magnolia denudata*, the 'Yulan' and *Magnolia liliiflora*, this is probably the most popular and widely planted of all Magnolias. It is variable in habit and flower colour and several clones have been given names. Multi-stemmed and eventually wide spreading (to 10 m or more), they flower before the leaves in April. 'Alba Superba' is almost pure white; 'Alexandrina' is erect with purple-flushed flowers crowding the branches; 'Lennei' is late (May) and dark rose-purple; 'Rustica Rubra' is a rich rosy-red and long-flowering whilst 'Picture' is erect in habit and bears huge purple-flushed flowers.

Magnolia virginiana

S

The "Sweet Bay" was probably the first magnolia to be grown in England, having been introduced from the eastern USA in the late seventeenth century. It is a useful tree of quiet charm, with often long persistent leaves glossy green above and blue-white beneath. The globular creamy-white flowers are rather small but sweetly scented and produced over a long period from June to September. Hardy and happy on most soils, though preferring a moist but well-drained loam.

MALUS

With the possible exception of Prunus, the "Ornamental Crabs" offer more trees suitable for the small garden than any other genus. Some are grown for flower, some for fruit, while others offer coloured foliage or autumn tints. As a group they are amenable to most soils and situations, flowering best in full sun.

Malus floribunda. An old specimen showing the floriferous habit of one of the most popular and reliable crabs.

Malus floribunda

S   **AGM 1923**

A round-headed tree transformed, at the end of April, into a mound of pale-blush flowers which crowd the arching branches and are crimson in bud. The small fruits which follow are yellow. It is a familiar tree in many gardens and is utterly reliable. It originated in Japan and is probably a hybrid.

Malus 'Golden Hornet'

S   **AGM 1969**

There are several yellow-fruited crabs, but if only one was to be chosen it should be this. The white flowers in April are replaced by rich golden-yellow, globular or conical fruits which thickly cluster the ascending branches, persisting until December to warm winter's cold breath.

Malus hupehensis

S–M   **AGM 1930**

This splendid crab has several things to offer, the first of which is its grey and brown flaking older bark. In April the stiffly ascending branches are wreathed in sweetly scented, white flowers, pink in bud, a tree in full flower resembling a snow-cloud from a distance. The fruits which follow are small and yellow, tinged with red. It is a native of both China and Japan. In the former country its leaves were once used for making tea.

Malus 'John Downie'

S   **AGM 1969**

Together with 'Golden Hornet' this is the most popular of the fruiting crabs for small gardens. The pink-budded white flowers in late May are followed by comparatively large, conical, bright orange and red fruits. These are of good flavour and may be used in preserves.

Malus 'Profusion'

S **AGM 1969**

Trees with red or purple foliage are not everyone's cup of tea, but in this tree the colour is mainly restricted to the young foliage which is coppery crimson fading to bronze-green. The wine-red, slightly fragrant flowers are 3–4 cm across and thickly clothe the branches in spring to be followed by small, oxblood-red fruits. It is perhaps the best of the coloured-leaf crabs.

Malus 'Red Sentinel'

S

In this tree the white flowers in early May are succeeded by attractive deep-red fruits 2·5 cm across which are borne along the branches in large clusters and persist long into winter, a most useful asset on a cold dreary December or January day.

Malus 'Profusion'. *Perhaps the best and most reliable of the red-flowered crabs.*

Malus 'Golden Hornet'. *The best yellow-fruited crab for general planting.*

Malus x robusta. A reliable fruiting crab.

Malus 'John Downie'. *One of the best fruiting crabs.*

Malus 'Profusion'.

Malus × *robusta*

S **AGM 1958**

This is a variable hybrid between *M. baccata* and *M. prunifolia*, with white or pink-flushed flowers in spring followed by red or yellow cherry-like fruits. The crab known as "Yellow Siberian" is a yellow-fruited clone of this hybrid and a fine garden tree.

Malus spectabilis

S

A most beautiful Chinese tree with upright branches, at least when young. These are decorated with large flowers, deep rose-red in bud, opening blush during late April and early May, fruits yellow. 'Riversii' is an equally beautiful clone with rose-pink, double flowers.

Malus transitoria

S

If I was to choose just one crab for all-round effect, it would be this beautiful Chinese species. Its slender arching branches produce a broad mushroom of a head clothed with prettily lobed leaves which are bright green in summer, turning butter-yellow in autumn. Added to this are the small but abundantly produced white flowers in May and the equally plentiful golden-yellow currant-like fruits in autumn. It is a tree of elegance and charm.

Malus trilobata

S

Although rarely seen, this splendid tree is one of the best for small gardens and restricted spaces and is thoroughly hardy and easy to grow. Its erect branches are clothed with deeply 3-lobed leaves which resemble those of a maple more than a crab. These become attractively tinted in autumn. The large white flowers appear clustered along the branches in May or early June. It is a native of the eastern Mediterranean region and northern Greece.

Malus tschonoskii

S–M

The best crab for the brilliance of its autumn colour, the bold foliage turning to yellow, orange, purple and scarlet. The white, pink-flushed flowers in May are followed by globular yellowish-green, purplish-tinted fruits. A popular Japanese tree much favoured by some authorities for street planting.

Malus 'Van Eseltine'

S

An ideal crab for the very small garden where its spire-like habit will not interfere with buildings and passers-by. The semi-double flowers up to 5 cm across are rose-scarlet in bud opening shell-pink and are followed by yellow fruits.

Malus tschonoskii. Lovely autumn leaves.

Malus 'Van Eseltine'. *Flowers in dense clusters.*

91

MORUS

A small genus of deciduous trees, the "Mulberries", while offering no beauty of flower, are, nevertheless, of great interest and are attractive both in leaf and autumn colour. Growing best in the warmer, southern areas of the British Isles they are happy in most soils, particularly those of a rich nature and are admirably suited to city and town gardens and those by the sea. Their roots are rather brittle, therefore great care should be taken when planting and only small specimens should be moved from the open ground.

Morus alba 'Pendula'

VS–S

A most effective weeping tree with long, densely packed, greyish branches, often forming a curtain, and clothed with large, heart-shaped, pale-green leaves which turn yellow in autumn. The "White Mulberry", of which this is a form, is the tree on whose leaves the silkworm is fed.

Morus nigra

S

The widespreading, heavily branched "Black Mulberry" is a familiar tree in old college and cathedral gardens. It lives to a great age, in time becoming gnarled, picturesque, and of great architectural value. Its dark-green, heart-shaped leaves are rough to the touch above, and the dark purplish-red fruits in autumn are edible and agreeable to the taste. In the wild it is a native of western Asia, but is known to have been cultivated in England since the early sixteenth century.

Morus nigra. The mulberry has rich historical associations.

Morus alba 'Pendula'. *A famous old specimen in Kew Gardens.*

NOTHOFAGUS

Sometimes referred to as "Southern Beech" the members of this small but ornamental genus are related to Fagus, *differing, among other things, in their normally smaller leaves. Some species are evergreen and most are fast-growing, but, unlike the "Common Beech", they are not very wind-resistant and are not suitable as screens or shelterbelts. They prefer a deep, moist but well-drained soil, and will not tolerate shallow chalk soils. Though relatively hardy, they seem best suited for the south and south-west of England.*

Nothofagus betuloides.

Nothofagus obliqua. A 19 year old tree showing extremely elegant habit.

Nothofagus betuloides

M
An evergreen species of dense compact habit. The small, leathery, toothed leaves are dark shining green in colour and are densely but neatly arranged on the closely packed branches. It is a native of Chile.

Nothofagus obliqua

L
The "Roblé Beech" is one of the fastest-growing and most elegant of hardy deciduous trees, its branches often gracefully drooping at their tips. The leaves are larger than in most species and are uneven at the base. It quickly develops into a beautiful specimen and makes an ideal specimen tree for a large lawn. It is a native of Chile.

NYSSA

This small genus contains at least two of the finest trees grown for autumn colour. Both flowers and fruit are insignificant. They require a moist, lime-free soil and, once established, resent disturbance, therefore they should be planted as young as possible.

Nyssa sylvatica. Glorious in autumn

Nyssa sylvatica. Leaves just turning in autumn.

Nyssa sylvatica

M–L   **AGM 1969**

The mound-like or broadly columnar shapes of the "Tupelo" in autumn dress are the pride and joy of several gardens in the south and west of England. At this season the dark glossy leaves are drained of their summer green and the whole tree erupts into a colourful bonfire of yellow, orange and scarlet. In the wild it occurs through eastern North America.

TREES WITH ATTRACTIVE FRUIT

Ailanthus altissima (female)
Alnus cordata
Arbutus x andrachnoides
Arbutus unedo
Castanea sativa
Catalpa bignonioides
Cercis siliquastrum
Cornus controversa
Cornus kousa
Cornus nuttallii
Cotoneaster frigidus
Cotoneaster ' Hybridus Pendulus '
Cotoneaster x watereri
Crataegus crus-galli
Crataegus laciniata
Crataegus prunifolia
Crataegus tanacetifolia
Fraxinus ornus
Gleditsia triacanthos
Idesia polycarpa (female)
Ilex x altaclarensis ' Camelliifolia '
Ilex x altaclarensis ' Golden King '
Ilex x altaclarensis ' Silver Sentinel '
Ilex x altaclarensis ' Lawsoniana '

Ilex aquifolium ' Handsworth New Silver '
Ilex aquifolium ' J.C. van Tol '
Ilex aquifolium ' Madame Briot '
Ilex aquifolium ' Pendula '
Ilex aquifolium ' Pyramidalis '
Koelreuteria paniculata
Magnolia acuminata
Malus ' Golden Hornet '
Malus ' John Downie '
Malus transitoria
Malus x robusta
Ostrya carpinifolia
Prunus lusitanica
Pterocarya fraxinifolia
Rhus trichocarpa (female)
Rhus typhina (female)
Sorbus aucuparia & cvs.
Sorbus cashmiriana
Sorbus hupehensis
Sorbus hybrida
Sorbus intermedia
Sorbus ' Joseph Rock '
Sorbus x kewensis
Sorbus scalaris
Sorbus vilmorinii

OSTRYA

*A small genus of hardy deciduous trees, closely related to and resembling the "Hornbeams" (*Carpinus*). They are elegant trees of easy cultivation on most soils.*

Ostrya carpinifolia

M

The "Hop Hornbean" is, perhaps, most pleasing in spring when its spreading branches are hung with the numerous, long, yellow, male catkins. The sharply toothed leaves give attractive yellow tints in autumn when they are accompanied by the curiously attractive hop-like fruit clusters. A native of southern Europe and western Asia.

Ostrya carpinifolia.
An easy-to-grow elegant tree.

OXYDENDRUM

A genus of only one species from the eastern USA. It requires a moist, lime-free soil and succeeds in sun or shade.

Oxydendrum arboreum

S–M   **AGM 1947**

The pleasant acid flavour of the leaves give this species its common name of "Sorrel Tree". These same leaves, which are long and dark green, turn to exquisite shades of yellow, crimson and purple in autumn. In July and August the long drooping racemes of white flowers emerge in clusters from the ends of the shoots, remaining effective for several weeks.

Oxydendrum arboreum. Few trees equal this for autumn tints.

Oxydendrum arboreum.
A young specimen in autumn.

PARROTIA

Rich autumn colour is the main feature of this interesting genus of which only a single species is known. It is a member of the same family as the "Witch Hazel" (Hamamelis) and is surprisingly lime-tolerant, although it thrives and colours best in a moist but well-drained soil, preferably in full sun.

Parrotia persica. Spring foliage.

Parrotia persica

S   **AGM 1969**

In cultivation this hardy deciduous tree normally forms a mound of wide-spreading branches on a short, thick, piebald trunk. It therefore requires plenty of elbow-room in which to develop. In autumn the deep-green leaves change to fiery scarlet and gold, when a big specimen presents a breathtaking sight. The tiny reddish flower-clusters in late winter often create a warm haze from a distance. Native of northern Iran and the Caucasus. On the wet hillsides above the Caspian Sea *Parrotia* is plentiful and forms forests together with hornbeam. In these forests trees are erect, often over 20 m high, and are late in colouring, usually December or January.

Parrotia persica. Rich autumn tints

Parrotia persica. The ' piebald ' stems in winter

PAULOWNIA

A small genus of deciduous trees thriving in most soils so long as they are reasonably well drained. They flower best in a warm sunny position sheltered from cold winds and, if possible, late frosts.

Paulownia tomentosa

S–M

A fast-growing, openly branched tree bearing stout downy shoots and oppositely arranged leaves which are large, usually 5-lobed, and downy beneath. The beautiful heliotrope-blue flowers, shaped like those of a foxglove, are 3·5–5 cm long. They are borne in terminal panicles and, though formed in autumn, do not open until the following May. Young sucker shoots grow prodigiously and produce leaves up to 1 m across. Large leaves may be encouraged by hard pruning of the previous year's shoots in March. It is a native of China, giving the best results in regions where both summer and winter climates are consistent.

Paulownia tomentosa.
A fast-growing, wide-spreading tree

PHILLYREA

A small genus of evergreen trees with opposite leaves. They are hardy, tolerant of most soils and situations, including polluted atmosphere and coastal blasts.

Phillyrea latifolia

S

For those who admire the billowy, dark-green foliage of the "Evergreen Oak" (*Quercus ilex*) but cannot find the necessary space, this tree is the ideal substitute. It is a native of southern Europe and western Asia and develops a dense rounded head with small, toothed leaves.

Phillyrea latifolia
A fine old specimen
of this useful evergreen tree

PLATANUS

A very distinct and highly ornamental genus of deciduous trees, resembling the "Maples" (Acer) in their palmately-lobed leaves which, however, are arranged alternately on the shoots. They are fast-growing when young and tolerant of most soils, though slower and least happy on shallow chalk soils.

Platanus orientalis 'Insularis'. Attractive fingered foliage.

Platanus x hispanica 'Suttneri'.
A striking variegation particularly on young foliage.

Platanus × hispanica

L

The "London Plane" is well known to most people, even to non-gardeners, and is one of the most commonly planted and most successful hardy trees in our towns and cities. No tree suffers pollution, mutilation and lack of care as well as this, and yet if it were to suffer the same fate as the "English Elm" the whole of London would be up in arms. Its familiar flaking, piebald trunk and branches are especially effective in winter when, at the same time, the branches are hung with the curious strings of bauble-like fruits. Its origin is a long-standing source of debate among botanists and others, but it is generally considered to be a hybrid between the "Oriental Plane" and the American "Buttonwood" (*P. occidentalis*).

Platanus × hispanica 'Suttneri'

L

A striking tree in which the leaves are boldly splashed and streaked creamy white and pink tinged when young, turning green as they mature.

Platanus orientalis

L

Equally large and requiring as much, if not more, space as the "London Plane" is the "Oriental Plane". Just as handsome, this species differs from the other mainly in its deeper-lobed leaves. It is said to be very long-lived, and in south-eastern Europe and western Asia where it occurs wild, there are many trees claimed to be of great antiquity. In northern Iran it withstands long hot summers followed by cold freezing winters.

Platanus orientalis insularis

M

This is a smaller tree than the type, with smaller, more deeply lobed and elegant leaves.

98

Platanus x hispanica. The tracery of branches against a sky at Exbury Gardens in spring

POPULUS

The "Poplars" are a large and varied genus of easy cultivation. The majority are hardy deciduous trees growing well in most soils except shallow chalk soils. They are especially useful for planting in wet areas and are often found in the wild by rivers and streams. Very fast-growing, with rapidly expanding crowns and vigorous greedy roots, they should not be planted near buildings or underground water or drainage pipes or, indeed, wherever water is not freely available. Catkins are produced, male and female on separate trees, those of the latter, when ripe, scattering cotton-woolly seeds which sometimes cause annoyance and frustration to city people.

Populus candicans ' Aurora '. Young trees in the nursery

Populus alba. A young tree showing white young growths

Populus alba

L

A suckering species, the "White Poplar" bears white-woolly-backed leaves which are 3–5-lobed on vigorous shoots and toothed elsewhere. These are effective when blowing in a wind and turn yellow in autumn. In this country the smooth bark is greyish in colour while in countries like Iran, where the atmosphere is drier, the bark gleams silvery white and is quite outstanding. It is a native of Europe and western Asia, occasionally naturalised but not wild in the British Isles. A form with yellow leaves is known as 'Richardii'.

Populus candicans 'Aurora'

M

This striking form of the "Balm of Gilead Poplar" produces stout angled shoots and broad heart-shaped leaves which are strongly balsam-scented when unfolding, scenting the air around. In colour they are boldly variegated creamy white and pink tinged when young, gradually turning green as they mature. It is a poplar counterpart to *Platanus × hispanica* 'Suttneri' and is perhaps best hard pruned each or every other year in February to encourage the coloured young foliage.

100

Populus nigra ' Plantierensis '. *An imposing column*

Populus lasiocarpa

M

The stout hairy twigs of this spectacular Chinese poplar carry heart-shaped, red-stalked leaves which may be as much as 30 cm long or more.

Populus 'Serotina Aurea'

L

The "Golden Poplar" is a most effective tree of vigorous growth. The heart-shaped leaves are bright yellow in spring and early summer, fading to yellow-green in summer and brightening to golden yellow before they fall in autumn. It is a male tree with a strong, openly branched head. If so desired, young trees may be hard pruned each or every other year in February to encourage the coloured young foliage and to control the size of the crown.

Populus lasiocarpa. A handsome poplar with large leaves.

Populus ' Serotina Aurea '. A young tree in late summer hard pruned every other year to produce a manageable crown

Populus nigra 'Italica'

L

Whether planted singly, in groups or in rows the "Lombardy Poplar" is an easily recognised tree in the landscape and few other trees match it for its sentinel-like effect. As its name suggests, it is Italian in origin and is mainly represented in cultivation by a male tree. Before planting this tree it should be remembered that its great height is matched by its vigorous root system.

Populus nigra 'Plantierensis'

L

A robust tree of tall columnar habit, broader than the "Lombardy Poplar", of which it is thought to be a hybrid. It is of French origin.

Populus 'Robusta'

L

One of the characteristics of this vigorous poplar is its straight main stem continuing to the summit, even when old. In spring the young leaves are an attractive coppery red becoming green later. It is a male tree and very popular, especially for screening purposes.

Populus tremula ' Pendula '. A 14 year old tree

Populus tremula. Bark detail.

Populus 'Robusta'.
Strong growing with coppery foliage in spring.

Populus tremula

S–M

The "Aspen" is mainly known for its rounded, prettily scalloped grey-green leaves which, because of their slender flattened stalks tremble in the slightest breeze. It is a suckering tree, often forming a thicket if allowed and draping its branches in February with delightful long grey catkins. The leaves turn to butter-yellow in autumn. In the wild it is distributed throughout Europe to western Asia and North Africa.

Populus tremula 'Pendula'

S

The "Weeping Aspen" forms a mushroom-shaped head of gracefully weeping branches and makes an attractive tree for grass areas where its suckering habit can be controlled by frequent close mowing.

103

PARTICULAR INTEREST OF LEAVES

Variegated Leaves

Acer negundo ' Elegans '
Acer negundo ' Variegatum '
Acer platanoides ' Drummondii '
Acer pseudoplatanus ' Leopoldii '
Cornus controversa ' Variegata '
Ilex x altaclarensis ' Golden King '
Ilex x altaclarensis ' Lawsoniana '
Ilex x altaclarensis ' Silver Sentinel '
Ilex aquifolium (several)
Ligustrum lucidum ' Excelsum Superbum '
Liquidambar styraciflua ' Aurea '
Liriodendron tulipifera ' Aureomarginatum '
Platanus x hispanica ' Suttneri '
Populus candicans ' Aurora '
Prunus lusitanica ' Variegata '
Quercus cerris ' Variegata '
Ulmus procera ' Argenteovariegata '

Red or Purple Leaves

Acer platatanoides ' Crimson King '
Acer platanoides ' Schwedleri '
Acer pseudoplatanus purpureum (leaves beneath
Catalpa x erubescens ' Purpurea ' *(when young)*
Fagus sylvatica purpurea
Fagus sylvatica ' Purpurea Pendula '
Malus ' Profusion '
Prunus cerasifera ' Nigra '
Prunus cerasifera ' Pissardii '
Prunus x blireana

Golden or Yellow Leaves

Acer cappadocicum ' Aureum '
Acer pseudoplatanus ' Worleei '
Alnus incana ' Aurea '
Alnus glutinosa ' Aurea '
Catalpa bignonioides ' Aurea '
Fagus sylvatica ' Zlatia ' *(when young)*
Populus alba ' Richardii '
Populus ' Serotina Aurea '
Quercus robur ' Concordia '
Quercus rubra ' Aurea ' *(when young)*
Robinia pseudoacacia ' Frisia '
Tilia x europaea ' Wratislaviensis ' *(when young)*
Ulmus x hollandica ' Wredei '
Ulmus x sarniensis ' Dicksonii '

Grey or Silver Leaves

Acer saccharinum (leaves beneath)
Crataegus laciniata
Crataegus tanacetifolia
Eucalyptus coccifera
Eucalyptus dalrympleana
Eucalyptus gunnii
Eucalyptus niphophila
Eucalyptus parvifolia
Fraxinus velutina
Populus alba
Populus tremula
Pyrus nivalis
Pyrus salicifolia ' Pendula '
Salix alba
Salix alba ' Sericea '
Sorbus aria (especially in spring)
Sorbus cuspidata
Tilia petiolaris (leaves beneath)
Tilia tomentosa (leaves beneath)

Autumn Colour of Leaf

Acer cappadocicum
Acer ginnala
Acer griseum
Acer platanoides
Acer rubrum especially
    ' Schlesingeri '
Acer saccharinum
Amelanchier lamarckii
Betula (all)
Carpinus (all)
Cercidiphyllum japonicum
Crataegus prunifolia
Fagus (all)
Fraxinus excelsior ' Jaspidea '
Fraxinus oxycarpa ' Raywood '
Ginkgo biloba
Liquidambar styraciflua
Malus transitoria
Malus trilobata
Malus tschonoskii
Morus alba ' Pendula '
Nyssa sylvatica

Ostrya carpinifolia
Parrotia persica
Populus alba
Populus ' Serotina Aurea '
Populus tremula
Prunus x hillieri ' Spire '
Prunus incisa
Prunus sargentii
Quercus coccinea especially
    ' Splendens '
Quercus rubra
Rhus trichocarpa
Rhus typhina
Sassafras albidum
Sorbus alnifolia
Sorbus ' Joseph Rock '
Sorbus scalaris
Stewartia (all)
Tilia mongolica
Ulmus (all)
Zelkova serrata

Trees with deeply cut or divided leaves

Acer japonicum ' Aconitifolium '
Acer saccharinum ' Laciniatum '
Aesculus (all)
Alnus glutinosa ' Imperialis '
Aralia elata
Betula pendula ' Dalecarlica '
Fagus sylvatica ' Asplenifolia '
Fraxinus (all)
Gleditsia triacanthos
Juglans nigra
Koelreuteria paniculata

Malus transitoria
Platanus orientalis insularis
Pterocarya fraxinifolia
Robinia (all)
Rhus trichocarpa
Rhus typhina (especially
    ' Laciniata ')
Sophora japonica
Sorbus (aucuparia group)
Tilia platyphyllos ' Laciniata '

Trees with scented flowers

Aesculus hippocastanum
Crataegus monogyna
Drymis winteri
Eucryphia x intermedia
Eucryphia milliganii
Laburnum alpinum
Magnolia grandiflora
Magnolia x loebneri
  ' Leonard Messel '
Magnolia virginiana
Malus floribunda

Malus ' Profusion '
Prunus ' Amanogawa '
Prunus lusitanica
Prunus ' Shirotae '
Prunus x yedoensis
Robinia pseudoacacia and cvs.
Styrax japonica
Tilia x euchlora
Tilia x europaea
Tilia petiolaris
Tilia platyphyllos

PRUNUS

Members of this large genus are, perhaps, the most commonly planted of all ornamental trees. Indeed it would be difficult to find a single row of gardens in which at least one flowering cherry, plum or almond was not represented. The popularity of Prunus lies in the presence of so many hardy, easy-to-grow trees suitable for small gardens. They are a varied throng and include several distinct groups such as cherries, plums, almonds, peaches and laurels. Collectively, they are unfussy as to soil as long as it is not waterlogged, although it is apparent that many of them, especially the "Japanese Cherries", actually thrive on shallow chalk soils, in which situations they often flower magnificently. They demand full sun for flowering but several are quite tolerant of shade. These include the laurels, which are among the best subjects for such situations. Apart from their floral attributes, many of the cherries also give rich autumn leaf tints.

Prunus dulcis. The ' Almond ' *flowering in early spring*

Prunus dulcis. The almond in flower.

Prunus persica 'Klara Mayer'. *The best and most reliable flowering peach.*

Prunus 'Kiku-shidare Sakura'. *Perhaps the best weeping cherry for small gardens.*

Prunus 'Amanogawa'

S   **AGM 1931**

One of the best of the "Japanese Cherries" for small gardens. The large erect clusters of fragrant, single or semi-double, shell-pink flowers appear in late April–early May among the greenish-bronze young foliage. A column of flower is a splendid sight on a sunny spring day. In autumn the leaves turn to yellow. It is normally grown "feathered" with branches to the base.

Prunus avium

M

The "Wild Cherry" or "Gean" is the commonest of our two native cherries, although in many areas it has been planted and become naturalised. It is conspicuous during late April–early May when the clusters of white cup-shaped flowers hang along the boughs. The leaves often turn red in autumn.

Prunus avium 'Plena'

M   **AGM 1924**

This splendid tree has all the qualities of the type but the white flowers are double and, as a consequence, are longer-lasting. It is a favourite cherry for parks and roadsides.

Prunus × *blireana*

S   **AGM 1928**

Wherever this tree is planted it never fails to cause comment when, in late March or early April, the slender branches are wreathed in double, rose-pink flowers which are slightly fragrant and 2·5 cm or more across. The effect is of a striking pink cloud, highlighted by the emergence of coppery-purple foliage. It is an ideal tree for the small garden and originated in France as a hybrid between the familiar "Purple-leaved Plum" *Prunus cerasifera* 'Pissardii' and *P. mume* 'Alphandii'.

Prunus cerasifera 'Nigra'

S

For lovers of purple foliage this is probably one of the best sources. The leaves and stems are a blackish purple, a very dark background for the small but abundantly produced pink flowers in late March and early April.

Prunus cerasifera 'Pissardii'

S   AGM 1928

"Purple-leaved Plum". Probably the commonest purple-leaved tree in cultivation, this was originally found sometime before 1880 by a M. Pissard, gardener to the Shah of Persia. The small pink-budded, white flowers appear in profusion along the slender branches in late March and early April when they are effectively backed by the emerging dark red turning to purple foliage.

Prunus dulcis

S

The "Almond" is one of the hardiest, earliest and most reliable of spring-flowering trees. Though rather open in branching, its clear pink flowers, 2·5–5 cm across, seen against a blue March or early April sky are unforgettable. The fruits when produced are rarely as satisfactory as those sold in shops, which are mainly imported from southern Europe. In the wild it occurs from North Africa to western Asia but is extensively naturalised in the Mediterranean region.

Prunus × hillieri 'Spire'

S

Probably one of the best small trees raised this century. Its shape makes it ideally suited to small gardens and confined spaces. The soft pink flowers crowd the branches in April, while in autumn the leaves turn a rich red. This tree is equally effective with its branches retained to the base as it is trained to a single stem.

Prunus incisa

S   AGM 1930

The "Fuji Cherry" is a densely branched tree with small, jaggedly toothed leaves often providing rich autumn tints. In late March or early April the slender branches are inundated with small pink-budded white flowers creating a pink haze from a distance. It is a tough, hardy cherry and has been used as a hedge as well as for bonsai culture. It is native to Japan. 'Praecox' is a selected clone flowering from January onwards, while 'February Pink' has deeper coloured flowers.

Prunus cerasifera 'Pissardii'. One of the most effective trees with purple leaves.

Prunus 'Kiku-shidare Sakura'.
The best small weeping cherry.

Prunus 'Kanzan'

S   AGM 1930

This must be just about the most commonly planted of all flowering cherries, and while some people regard it as vulgar and overplanted, its popularity continues. The stiffly ascending branches are characteristic of its early years, becoming spreading later. In late April and early May specimens of this tree become immediately noticeable when the branches are smothered by rich, hanging bunches of large, double flowers which are a distinctive purplish pink in colour at first, becoming pink later. It is a colour and effect which some people find garish but others see as the epitome of a flowering tree.

Prunus 'Kiku-shidare Sakura'

S

Perhaps the best weeping cherry for small gardens, its branches wreathed, during April, with double rose-pink flowers, like the pink button chrysanthemums. The leaves are bronze-green on emerging, becoming glossy green later.

Prunus 'Kanzan'. *The most popular of all cherries.*

Prunus lusitanica

S–M

The "Portugal Laurel" is one of the very few evergreen species of *Prunus* and to the casual eye bears no resemblance to the cherries or plums except when in flower or fruit. The leaves are dark glossy green with red stalks and, though dark in effect, are brightened in June by the numerous slender racemes of small hawthorn-scented white flowers. These are replaced by juicy red, turning to shining black, small, cherry-like fruits. A native of Spain and Portugal this hardy tree is amenable to most soils and situations, including shallow chalk soils and dense shade.

Prunus lusitanica 'Variegata'

S

A pretty form with attractive creamy-white variegated leaves, often pink tinged during winter. Unforunately, it is less hardy than the type and should be given shelter from cold winds.

Prunus 'Mikuruma-gaeshi'

S

A very distinctive cherry with its long ascending branches, presenting a gaunt appearance when not in flower. This is suddenly changed in mid-April when the same branches become long arms of single blush-pink flowers scented of apple-blossom. The foliage is bronze-green on emerging, turning a rich coppery red and yellow in autumn. Because of its upright habit this is a good cherry for planting by paths or boundary hedges.

Prunus persica

S

Flowering in April two to three weeks later than the "Almond", the "Peach" possesses similar but smaller pink single flowers borne in clusters along the naked stems. The young shoots are typically green, conspicuous in winter, and the flowers are followed by juicy fruits which, however, do not compare with those sold in shops. These are produced by selected fruiting clones. As a native tree it probably originated from China, although it has been cultivated from time immemorial and is naturalised in many regions of southern Europe and Asia. There are now available many named cultivars, varying mainly in flower colour.

Prunus persica 'Cardinal'

S

A charming tree with semi-double rosette-like flowers of a glowing red. 'Russell's Red' is an old cultivar with double crimson flowers and is still the best of its colour.

Prunus persica 'Iceberg'

S

A free-flowering form with exquisite, large semi-double flowers of pure white. 'Alboplena' is an older cultivar with flowers of similar form and colour.

Prunus persica 'Klara Mayer'

S **AGM 1939**

This is perhaps the best double peach for general cultivation. Its flowers are a beautiful peach-pink and crowd the branches. 'Prince Charming' has double rose-red flowers.

Prunus sargentii

S **AGM 1928**

Without doubt this is one of the finest of all trees grown for autumn colour. In late March or early April the spreading branches become crowded with single bright-pink flowers which are later joined by the coppery-red young foliage. As autumn approaches this is one of the first trees, and certainly the first cherry to colour, usually in mid to late September. Not only is its autumn display rich in orange and crimson tints, but it is reliable and regular, whatever the weather. It is native to Japan, Sakhalin and Korea.

Prunus lusitanica 'Variegata'. *A useful variegated evergreen for more sheltered gardens.*

Prunus serrula. Superb polished bark.

Prunus serrula

S

A native of western China this desirable cherry is one of the many ornamental trees introduced by that great plant collector Ernest Wilson. Unlike most other cherries this species is not planted for its flowers but for its bark. The white flowers are not only small but appear with and are virtually concealed by the narrow willow-like leaves in April. The bark on the trunk and branches, however, more than makes up for the lack of floral beauty. In colour it is dark shining coppery brown and peels prettily to reveal the highly polished mahogany-red new bark. This is highly effective and attractive at all times, especially so during winter when the garden offers few if any counter attractions. The brilliance and shine of the trunk is encouraged by constant rubbing, and I once knew a gardener who always invited visitors to give his tree a vigorous patting and smoothing with the hands to help achieve this.

Prunus 'Shimidsu Sakura'

S   **AGM 1933**

A lovely cherry of distinct habit, forming a low, widespreading head of branches, in later life becoming rather flat-topped with the long branches gracefully drooping at the tips. As such it is a most effective lawn tree for the medium-sized or large garden. During May the large, fringed, double flowers hang in long-stalked clusters all along the boughs. They are pink flushed in bud, opening pure white, and resemble ballet-girls' skirts in their frilled effect. The young leaves are green and appear with the flowers, turning orange and red before falling in autumn.

Prunus 'Shirofugen'

S   **AGM 1959**

One of the best "Japanese Cherries" for general planting, being attractive in habit and generous in its flowering which is late and long-lasting. The Japanese name for this tree means "White God" and is certainly most appropriate. It is a vigorous tree with widespreading branches, the lower ones often pendulous with age. The large double flowers are purplish pink in bud, opening white and fading to purplish pink. They are produced in long-stalked clusters during May, hanging from the branches and contrasting effectively with the coppery-bronze young foliage. The leaves in autumn turn to deep orange and coppery brown.

Prunus subhirtella 'Pendula Rubra'. *Flowering in March and summer foliage.*

Prunus sargentii. One of the first trees to colour in autumn.

Prunus 'Shirotae'

S

Known as the "Mount Fuji Cherry" in reference to its snow-white flowers, this beautiful tree develops a comparatively low, wide habit with long horizontally spreading branches which become lax with age, their extremities often touching the ground. The very large fragrant flowers are semi-double or sometimes single especially on young trees. In colour they are a dazzling snow-white and hang in long-stalked clusters from the branches in late April when they are backed by the soft green, heavily fringed leaves. In a good autumn the leaves turn golden yellow.

Prunus subhirtella 'Autumnalis'

S   AGM 1924

During the normally dreary months from late autumn to early spring there exists a small nucleus of woody plants which dare to flower and bring colour into the garden. The "Autumn Cherry" is one of them. The small semi-double, pale-blush, frilled flowers first appear in November and continue to open during mild spells until the end of March. Most days during winter will find the slender, wand-like branches of this cherry clustered with flowers and, like most winter-blooming plants, it is useful for cutting and bringing a few sprigs into the home. In

autumn the leaves often turn a rich red and bronze, 'Autumnalis Rosea' has flowers of a deeper pink, while 'Fukubana' is perhaps the most colourful with flowers of rose-madder.

Prunus subhirtella 'Pendula Rosea'

S

A graceful mushroom-headed tree, ideal for the small garden. Its long, weeping, wand-like branches are sprinkled, during late March and early April, with small, single flowers which are pink in bud opening pale blush. The leaves often colour richly in autumn. 'Pendula Rubra' is an even more striking tree with flowers carmine in bud opening deep rose.

Prunus 'Tai Haku'

S   AGM 1964

The name "Great White Cherry" aptly describes this Japanese tree which has the distinction of having the largest flowers of any cherry, up to 6 cm across. These are borne in April and though pinkish in bud open to a dazzling white, contrasting superbly with the rich coppery-red young foliage. It is a strong-growing tree and one of the best cherries for general planting. The leaves turn yellow and orange in autumn.

Prunus 'Ukon'

S   AGM 1969

The unusual colour of the flowers of this robust cherry make it a popular choice for special effects and a favourite with flower arrangers. They are semi-double and pale yellowish in colour with a tinge of green, and an occasional pink flush. Borne in large clusters in late April and early May, they show up well against the brownish-bronze young foliage. In autumn the leaves turn to rusty red, bronze and purplish.

Prunus × yedoensis

S   AGM 1930

Unknown in the wild, the "Yoshino Cherry" originated in Japan and is generally thought to be a hybrid between *P. speciosa* and *P. subhirtella*. It is particularly valued for the profusion of its almond-scented, blush-white flowers before the leaves in late March or early April. The foliage often colours attractively in autumn.

Prunus 'Tai Haku'. Perhaps the largest flowered of all cherries.

PTEROCARYA

Only a few species represent this handsome and useful genus of deciduous trees. They belong to the "Walnut" family and, like these trees, have long pinnate leaves with numerous leaflets; the fruits, however, are winged and are borne in pendulous strings. They are suitable for most soils and bring a touch of the exotic to the garden or park.

Pterocarya fraxinifolia

L

A handsome suckering tree, generally developing a widespreading head when isolated, taller when growing with other trees. It is effective enough when in leaf and is even more so during summer when the long greenish catkins drape the branches. These are replaced by unusual and decorative green, winged fruits. It is a hardy, fast-growing tree especially suitable for wet places. In the river valleys south of the Caspian Sea I have seen this tree forming thickets and groves by the water's edge. It is native from the Caucasus to northern Iran.

Pterocarya fraxinifolia.
Handsome and hardy, excellent in moist situations.

PYRUS

A small genus of hardy deciduous trees suitable for most soils and tolerant of drought, maritime exposure and industrial pollution. Considering their values, just outlined, it is puzzling that the ornamental pears, save for the "Weeping Willow-leaved Pear", have never become more widely established in cultivation. All bear clusters of white flowers in April and several have attractive grey or silver foliage.

Pyrus nivalis

S

A most attractive silver-leaved tree. Native of southern Europe, its stout ascending branches are clothed in April with clusters of white flowers. At the same time the white-woolly young leaves emerge, turning grey later. The rounded greenish-brown fruits which follow are very hard, only becoming soft and edible when overripe. Eye-catching effects may be had by planting and training into this tree either the "Purple-leaved Vine" (*Vitis vinifera* 'Purpurea') or the "Golden-leaved Hop" (*Humulus lupulus* 'Aureus').

Pyrus salicifolia 'Pendula'

S   **AGM 1969**

"Weeping Willow-leaved Pear". The best known and most commonly planted ornamental pear, this elegant tree forms a dense mound of weeping branches clothed with silvery-grey, downy, narrow, willow-like leaves. Later in the season these become grey-green and smooth above. Flowers white in mid-April. The small fruits are top-shaped and brown in colour. A most effective combination may be achieved by planting the "Purple-leaved Vine" (*Vitis vinifera* 'Purpurea') to grow through the branches of this pear.

Pyrus ussuriensis

S–M

An elegant tree from north-eastern Asia, with glossy, green, slender pointed leaves turning bronze-crimson in autumn. The clusters of white flowers appear in early April and are replaced by small, hard, yellow-green fruits.

Pyrus salicifolia 'Pendula'. Mound of silvery foliage.

Pyrus nivalis. A most attractive silver-leaved tree.

113

QUERCUS

Quercus robur. The English Oak, part of a proud heritage.

The "Oaks" are a large and variable genus of deciduous and evergreen trees occurring both in cold temperate and tropical regions. As ornamental trees they have much to offer. Most are of noble proportions when mature and many are long-lived, some gathering legends true and false by the score. A number of the American oaks are known for their autumn colours, while others bear large and imposing leaves. The male and female flowers are borne separately on the same tree. Neither are of ornamental merit. Female flowers produce the well-known fruits — acorns. Those described here are relatively hardy and, unless indicated otherwise, are suitable for most soils and situations. None are really suitable for small gardens.

Quercus canariensis. The 'Algerian Oak' has almost evergreen foliage.

Quercus canariensis

L

Known as the "Algerian Oak", this fine, hardy, fast-growing species develops a rounded head of branches. The comparatively large, boldly lobed, dark-green leaves, paler beneath, thickly clothe the twigs, giving the crown a dense compact appearance. Even in winter the leaves seem reluctant to fall and not until the New Year do they finally succumb. This is a fast-growing oak happy on most soils, including those on chalk or heavy clay. It is a native of North Africa, southern Portugal and Spain.

Quercus castaneifolia

M–L

A native of north Iran and the Caucasus. I have seen the "Chestnut-leaved Oak" in the former country, growing in the forests above the Caspian Sea and in the Elburz Mountains behind, its dying foliage creating tall flames and mounds of copper and gold against the evening hillside. It is a fast-growing tree resembling the "Turkey Oak" in general appearance, with oblong, coarsely toothed, chestnut-like leaves of a dark shining green above, grey and downy beneath.

Quercus cerris

L

The "Turkey Oak", though a native of southern Europe and western Asia is commonly planted in the British Isles and has become naturalised in some areas. It is one of the fastest growing of all oaks and is an excellent screening tree, particularly in coastal areas. It is also excellent on dry chalk soils. The coarsely toothed or lobed leaves are glossy green and rough to the touch above.

Quercus cerris 'Variegata'

M–L

A rare form with leaves boldly margined and striped creamy white.

Quercus coccinea

L

One of the most spectacular large trees grown for autumn colour, the "Scarlet Oak" is a fast-growing tree when young, soon making a sizeable specimen of rather openly branched habit. The large, deeply and sharply lobed leaves are glossy green on both surfaces and in a good season turn a rich scarlet, the colour often developing in patches, almost branch by branch. It is a native of eastern North America and was introduced into cultivation as long ago as 1691. It is quite hardy and is suitable for all soils excepting chalk soils.

Quercus coccinea 'Splendens'

L   **AGM 1927**

Like all autumn-colour trees grown from seed, the "Scarlet Oak" is variable in effect and this clone is generally considered to be the best selection. It is grafted on to stocks of the common kind.

Quercus frainetto

L

Bold foliage is the chief attraction of the "Hungarian Oak". It is a relatively fast-growing tree, older specimens displaying a handsome, rugged, fissured bark. The large leaves are broad at the top, narrowing to the stalk and are deeply lobed with characteristic oblong lobes. It is hardy, and is excellent on all soils except those which are excessively wet. Native to south-eastern Europe.

Quercus cerris 'Variegata'. *An attractive form of the "Turkey Oak".*

Quercus coccinea 'Splendens'. *One of the glories of autumn.*

Quercus frainetto. The Hungarian Oak's *handsome lobed leaves.*

Quercus ilex

L

Although growing to a large size, few trees match the "Evergreen Oak" or "Holm Oak" for the lush piles of its evergreen foliage, which is especially effective in winter when all around is grey and bare. It is variable in leaf and those of young saplings can look very different from those of a mature specimen. Older trees develop a picturesque chequered grey bark, while the leathery leaves are generally narrow, dark glossy green above and grey downy beneath. In June the whole canopy is transformed by the emergence of white-woolly young shoots and clusters of pendulous yellow male catkins. Native of the Mediterranean region and south-western Europe, this majestic tree is suitable for most soils and situations, even tolerating shade and coastal gales. It is, however, subject to damage by frost in cold inland districts of the north.

Quercus robur

L

One cannot praise too highly the merits of our native "English Oak" which, despite its common name, is also found in the wild throughout Europe, the Caucasus, south-western Asia and North Africa. There is a danger that many people, with the necessary garden space, might disregard this oak as being common and not exotic nor exciting enough to be considered for planting. If this attitude were to become widely accepted it would be a sad day for England, and all other countries who once depended so much upon the oak. Its habit and growth are perhaps too familiar to need describing, but I must add that few trees inspire as much feeling in people as this. It is a strong and unshakeable part of our history and development, and there are many ancient specimens up and down the country, witnesses to the time when oak forest was more dominant in the land. The oak is one of several trees which we plant for posterity and I only hope that, in this often selfish epoch, we can, when circumstances permit, forget our preoccupation with the short-term values, at least enough to permit the planting of trees such as this.
Hardy and happy in most soils and situations, the "English Oak" has given rise to numerous unusual, as well as attractive variations.

Quercus ilex. The "Evergreen Oak" here seen as a young specimen.

116

Quercus robur 'Fastigiata'. *A young specimen of the "Cypress Oak".*

Quercus rubra.
Some forms colour richly in autumn.

Quercus x turneri. A splendid old specimen at Kew Gardens.

Quercus robur 'Concordia'

S

Slower-growing than the type, the "Golden Oak" is, when well developed, one of the most effective coloured-foliage trees. The leaves of this round-headed tree are golden yellow throughout spring and summer. Like the equally effective but faster-growing and larger "Golden Poplar" (*Populus* 'Serotina Aurea') it was raised at Van Geert's nursery at Ghent during the last century.

Quercus robur 'Fastigiata'

L

Known as the "Cypress Oak", this very useful tree is fastigiate in youth, broadening out and becoming broadly columnar as it matures. In time it reaches a considerable height and is an ideal tree for formal effects or to give height to otherwise low or horizontal plantings.

Quercus rubra

L

The "Red Oak" of eastern North America is easily one of the most vigorous and impressive of all hardy large trees. Given a lime-free soil it soon develops into a fine specimen with bold, sharply lobed leaves. These are normally dull green beneath and are capable of superb colouring in autumn. However, as most trees are normally seed-grown by the nurseryman, autumn colour is variable and while the leaves of some trees turn a rich red, those of other trees may turn yellow, or just brown before falling. It is a most adaptable tree and thrives in most situations, even in industrial areas. It is occasionally seen on the borders of conifer plantations on Forestry Commission land and makes an excellent specimen tree for the large garden or park.

Quercus rubra 'Aurea'

S–M

This unusual form of the "Red Oak" is mainly grown for its striking effect in spring when the emerging leaves appear a bright yellow, gradually turning to green as summer arrives. Although rare in cultivation it is one of the finest trees for spring effect.

Quercus × turneri

S–M

Known as "Turner's Oak", after the nurseryman who raised it at the end of the eighteenth century, this dense, round-headed tree is a hybrid between the "Evergreen Oak" (*Q. ilex*) and the "English Oak" (*Q. robur*). Its long, broadly toothed leaves are dark green above and thickly clothe the stems, creating an almost black-green effect from a distance. Though deciduous, the leaves remain on the branches until well in the New Year. It is a very hardy, tolerant and adaptable tree, especially good on shallow chalk soils.

Quercus velutina 'Rubrifolia'

L

Although not a common tree, "Champion's Oak" is quite hardy and easy to grow on all but chalk soils. It is also fast-growing and bears some of the largest and boldest leaves of all oaks. They are often hooded in appearance, dark shining green above, occasionally up to 40 cm long and are held rather loosely on the branches. The inner bark of this tree is bright yellow in colour and yields a yellow dye.

Quercus velutina ' Rubrifolia '
An 18 year old tree showing its handsome large leaves

RHUS

A large genus of deciduous trees, shrubs and climbers. Those trees in general cultivation are hardy and grown mainly for their handsome leaves which are pinnately divided into numerous leaflets, colouring richly in autumn. The flowers are normally inconspicuous, male and female being borne on separate trees. They are easily cultivated and generally unfussy as to soil. They are also tolerant of atmospheric pollution and are, therefore, good town and city trees.

Rhus trichocarpa

S

A most attractive Japanese tree of pleasing habit with long, downy ash-like leaves mainly gathered towards the ends of the branches. These are coppery pink when emerging, becoming rich green in summer and turning to a fiery scarlet or orange in autumn. A tree in early autumn contains some striking effects, with some leaves colouring and others still green.

Rhus typhina ' Laciniata :

Rhus trichocarpa. A 17 year old tree in autumn dress.

Rhus typhina

VS–S   AGM 1969

The "Stag's-horn Sumach" is perhaps one of the most frequently planted of all small trees in cities and town gardens, which is not surprising as it is "bone" hardy and easy to grow. In fact it is almost impossible not to succeed with this tree. Its broadly domed or flat-headed shape is a common feature in suburban gardens, particularly noticeable in autumn when the handsome leaves turn to red, scarlet, orange and yellow. Even in winter the gaunt, densely brown, felted stems are not without interest, especially those of female trees which retain tight terminal cones of dark-crimson, bristly fruits. It is prone to suckering, which need not be a bad thing, providing, as it does, ideal gift plants for friends. The previous year's shoots may be pruned hard back each or every other year in February to encourage strong young shoots bearing extra-large leaves, which, in the cultivar 'Laciniata', are deeply and attractively cut creating a fern-like effect. It is a native of eastern North America and is said to have first been cultivated as long ago as 1629.

ROBINIA

A small genus of deciduous trees and shrubs all native to North America. They are members of the "Pea" family and are closely related to Gleditsia, *the "Honey Locusts". Their leaves are divided into numerous leaflets like those of an ash, and their stems are often armed with hooked thorns. All are hardy and fast-growing, suitable for most soils and especially useful for dry or sandy soils. They are tolerant of atmospheric pollution and coastal conditions, but are not the best trees for windswept situations where they are prone to broken branches. Ideally they require a position in full sun for flowering.*

Robinia pseudoacacia 'Rozynskyana'.
The drooping leaves create a weeping appearance.

Robinia pseudoacacia 'Frisia'.
Now one of the most popular golden-foliaged trees.

Robinia × ambigua 'Decaisneana'

S–M   **AGM 1969**

A hybrid between the "False Acacia" (*R. pseudoacacia*) and the "Clammy Locust" (*R. viscosa*), this easy-to-grow and attractive tree was raised in France over a hundred years ago and is still very popular there, particularly as a street tree. In June the large pendulous clusters of pink flowers thrust their way through the foliage, creating a most pleasant picture.

Robinia × hillieri

S

One of the most satisfactory of the small tree robinias, developing a rounded head of slender branches and elegant leaves. The lilac-pink flowers are slightly fragrant and appear in nodding clusters in June. Like all "Robinias", its branches are brittle and are easily broken when exposed to strong winds. It is a hybrid between *R. kelseyi* and *R. pseudoacacia*.

Robinia pseudoacacia

M–L

Known as the "Common Acacia" or "False Acacia" this is one of the most vigorous and easiest to grow of all hardy trees. Once established it suckers prodigiously and will, if allowed, form dense thickets of thorny stems, hence its use as a soil binder in sandy areas. As a specimen tree it bears an impressive grooved and fissured bark and old trees often develop a picturesque gnarled and ancient appearance. The drooping clusters of white, slightly scented flowers appear along the branches in June and are very attractive to bees.

Robinia pseudoacacia 'Inermis'.
A popular tree for formal effect.

Robinia pseudoacacia 'Inermis'

S   **AGM 1969**

An easily recognised tree with its densely rounded head of spineless branches giving it the common name "Mop-head Acacia". It is rather formal in effect and is commonly planted as a street tree, particularly in France. It is liable to breakages in exposed or windy situations.

Robinia pseudoacacia 'Frisia'

S–M   **AGM 1969**

Raised in a Dutch nursery in 1935, this splendidly colourful foliage tree has, especially in the last ten years, become one of the most popular and desirable of all ornamental trees. Its foliage remains a striking golden yellow right through from spring until autum, a feature which makes it an important part of any garden colour scheme.

Robinia pseudoacacia 'Rozynskyana'

S

Under this rather laborious name we find a most elegant tree. The spreading branches droop at the tips, but it is the large drooping leaves which give this tree its almost weeping effect. The usual clusters of white flowers are produced in June.

SASSAFRAS

A small genus of deciduous trees of which only the following is in general cultivation. It requires a lime-free, moist but well-drained soil, preferably in the shelter of other trees.

Sassafras albidum

M

A hardy tree producing suckers when happily established. Its flowers are insignificant and the chief ornamental value of this tree, therefore, lies in its leaves which exhibit a startling range of shapes. They vary from oval and entire to 3-lobed, all variations appearing on the one tree. In colour they are bright green above and blue-green below, turning a lovely butter-yellow in autumn. Even when leafless in winter the tree displays a rugged fissured bark and wavy twigs and branches. Belonging to the "Bay" family, all parts of the tree are aromatic, and in its native eastern North America the bark and roots are sometimes used to make Sassafras tea.

Sassafras albidum. Leaves of peculiar shapes.

SALIX

The "Willows" are a very large and diverse genus of deciduous trees and shrubs, most of which are hardy and of the easiest cultivation. Indeed, some species, in common with the poplar, are extremely vigorous and rapidly develop into a large size and, therefore should not be planted near buildings or underground drains. Others, however, are smaller and quite suitable for more humble gardens. Apart from their vigour and ability to grow on a variety of soils, particularly those of a wet nature, many of the willows are notable for their display of male catkins in late winter or early spring, while others have attractive coloured twigs in winter. In connection with the production of catkins it should be remembered that male and female catkins are borne on separate trees, and when buying for attractive catkins a male clone must be asked for.

Salix aegyptiaca

S   **AGM 1969**

In February and March the stout grey-felted shoots of this willow are decorated in the male form with conspicuous yellow catkins creating a cloud of welcome colour at the end of winter. It is a native of southern Russia and the mountains of Asia. In northern Iran I have seen it crowding the rivers which flow through the rugged Elburz Mountains, lighting the dark gulleys when all above was cold rock and snow.

Salix alba

L

The "White Willow" is one of the most familiar and easily recognised of our large native trees. It occurs in water meadows, by rivers, etc., and presents a great mound of narrow silver-backed leaves shimmering and flashing in the wind. It is an excellent tree for maritime exposure and is often used as a windbreak there. It is found wild through Europe to northern Asia and North Africa.

Salix alba 'Chermesina'

L

Although its summer foliage is pleasant enough, this cultivar is essentially a tree for winter effect when its brilliant orange-scarlet young stems lend warmth and much-needed colour to the bleak garden landscape. If allowed to develop unchecked it will soon make a tall tree, when the coloured twigs have to be admired from afar. Alternatively, as a young tree, it may be hard pruned each or every other year in February or March in order to encourage stronger and brighter new shoots enjoyable nearer eye level.

Salix alba 'Sericea'

M   **AGM 1969**

A slower-growing, smaller form of the "White Willow", with leaves of an intense silvery hue, very striking either close to or from a distance.

Salix alba 'Vitellina'

M   **AGM 1969**

A golden version of 'Chermesina', with young shoots coloured yoke-of-egg yellow. Like the other it may be hard pruned to encourage stronger, brighter growths.

Salix caprea 'Pendula'

E

Known as the "Kilmarnock Willow", this neat, umbrella-shaped tree is a weeping form of our native "Goat Willow" or "Pussy Willow" beloved by children for its silky "pussies" and its golden male catkins known as "Palm" in early spring. This pendulous version is a female clone and does not possess the brighter catkins but is, nevertheless, a most useful little tree for small gardens.

Salix × chrysocoma

M   **AGM 1931**

This beautiful tree is perhaps the most popular and commonly planted of all weeping trees. It is usually the one most people think of when they *picture* a weeping tree, the strongly arching branches splaying out long, slender, golden-yellow shoots which eventually hang down to touch the ground, forming attractive curtains. The effect is best seen during winter when the tree is naked, but even in summer, when clothed with slender, bright-green leaves, it presents an unforgettable picture. It is said to be a hybrid of *S. alba* 'Vitellina' with the original "Weeping Willow" (*S. babylonica*), and has now superseded the latter as a familiar riverside tree. Like most willows it is fast-growing and forms a widespreading head. It is, therefore, mainly suitable for large gardens and parks, and the temptation to plant it in small gardens, where it is all too frequently seen, should be resisted. One shadow lies over this willow and that is its susceptibility to scab and canker, a disfiguring disease which is only practicably controlled on a small, young tree.

Salix alba 'Sericea'.
The most satisfactory willow for silvery foliage

Salix x chrysocoma. Now commonly planted

Salix alba 'Chermesina'.
Excellent when hard pruned for winter effect.

Salix caprea 'Pendula'.
The strongly weeping crown in summer.

Salix daphnoides

S   **AGM 1969**

If only one willow tree could be included in the garden perhaps the "Violet Willow" would be the best choice. Its vigorous upright shoots are deep purple in colour and are covered by a white plum-like bloom which can be rubbed off with the finger. If a male clone, such as 'Aglaia' is acquired, one can also enjoy the large yellow catkins which appear before the leaves in late winter or early spring. In order to enhance the winter display, the branches may be hard pruned each or every other year in February or March thereby encouraging the production of strong, heavily bloomed, young shoots. Its leaves are a handsome polished dark green above, blue-white below. In the wild it ranges from northern Europe to central Asia.

Salix matsudana

M

A graceful tree of pleasingly neat habit, the slender stems clothed with narrow leaves, green above, grey beneath. Known as the "Pekin Willow" it is native of northern China, Manchuria and Korea, and is an excellent willow for dry soils and cold barren areas.

Salix matsudana 'Tortuosa'. *An attractive tree of unusual form equally effective in winter.*

Salix matsudana 'Pendula'

S–M

If a beautiful, not-too-large weeping willow is required for the garden, none would better this tree. Its long slender branches arch and weep in a most graceful fashion and appear even more ethereal in spring when spattered with the bright-green tufts of the emerging leaves. Though less spectacular than $S. \times chrysocoma$ it does have the important advantage of being scab and canker resistant.

Salix matsudana 'Tortuosa'

M

One of the most striking and easily recognised willows because of the curious twisting and spiralling of its branches and shoots. It provides one of the best talking-points in any garden, especially during winter when its strange growth is seen to best advantage.

Salix purpurea

S

Occurring in the wild throughout Europe and into central Asia, the "Purple Osier" is one of our more graceful native species. Often shrubby in habit it may be trained up to a single stem, and its long, slender branches allowed to arch and splay out in all directions. In April the slender, often paired, catkins appear all along the stems and are later replaced by the narrow blue-green leaves. If the bark of the young shoots is scraped with the finger-nail the wood revealed will be a bright yellow. It is one of the most adaptable willows, being as good on dry soils as on wet, while its strong flexible stems are often used in basket-making.

Salix purpurea 'Eugenei'

S

This is, perhaps, the best form of the "Purple Osier", developing into a slender conical tree. It is a male clone and the pink-flushed grey catkins appearing along the erect branches in early spring add just that extra touch of charm.

Salix purpurea 'Pendula'

VS

The best weeping willow for small gardens, reproducing all the charm and elegance of the larger weepers on a miniature scale.

Salix matsudana 'Tortuosa'. *A superb tracery of contorted stems in winter.*

SOPHORA

Both evergreen and deciduous trees and shrubs are found in this interesting genus, though only the following species makes anything like a large tree in the British Isles.

Sophora japonica.
A handsome tree flowering only with age.

Sophora japonica 'Pendula'.
A young tree showing its neat weeping habit.

Sophora japonica

M–L

The "Pagoda Tree", although native of China, has long been cultivated in Japan and is very common there. It is a spectacular tree when mature, of bold rounded appearance with rugged bark, and with leaves divided into numerous leaflets like those of an ash. The creamy-white pea-flowers are borne in large terminal branched heads during late summer and autumn and, when finished, shower the ground below. Unfortunately, trees do not normally flower until at least 30 years of age. It thrives best in the drier eastern regions of the British Isles and requires a well-drained soil and plenty of sun to be seen at its best.

Sophora japonica 'Pendula'

S

Even without flowers this is a useful and attractive weeping tree, with long, stiffly pendulous branches, eventually reaching to the ground. It is best grown on a lawn where its cooling shade in summer may better be appreciated.

SORBUS

Second only to the "Cherries" (Prunus) and "Crabs" (Malus) as the most popular small garden trees, the many members of this large genus present a wide range of ornamental effects. Botanically they fall into two main groups, the "Whitebeams" and the "Mountain Ashes". The former are mainly grown for their attractive, often large, oval or rounded, greyish-green leaves which are covered in white down in spring. The mountain ashes, by far the larger group, bring rich autumn colouring of leaves and fruits, the former of which are divided like those of an ash. All species are hardy and deciduous, growing in a wide variety of soils and situations, and are tolerant of atmospheric pollution as well as coastal blasts. Compared with other, larger trees, they are not long lived but amply repay their keep with some of the most reliable and satisfying attractions in the gardening year. With few exceptions the species here described are erect in habit when young, widening out later and bear white flowers in may.

Sorbus alnifolia

S–M

This uncommon but desirable Japanese species is quite hardy and easy of cultivation. It develops a neat compact head of ascending branches densely clothed with sharply toothed leaves somewhat resembling those of "Hornbeam". These turn to a warm orange and scarlet in autumn when they are accompanied by bunches of small, oval, orange-red berries.

Sorbus aria

S–M **AGM 1969**

Our native "Whitebeam", a familiar tree of chalk downs in the south of England where it often jostles for space with the yew. It is an extremely tough, round-headed tree and is one of the few trees which is able to withstand fierce coastal winds as well as atmospheric pollution. Its rounded, toothed leaves are covered by a startling white down on emerging in spring, becoming grey-green and white-backed in summer, then

Sorbus aucuparia 'Beissneri'. Warm orange-coloured branches are a feature in drier eastern areas of the British Isles.

turning to russet and gold in autumn when they are joined by bunches of large deep-crimson, brown-speckled berries. The creamy-white flowers are produced in May. It is found as a native throughout Europe.

Sorbus aria 'Decaisneana'

S–M **AGM 1969**

A distinct and impressive form of "Whitebeam", of upright habit when young and bearing large leaves often 10–15 cm long. Even the deep-crimson berries in autumn are larger and more conspicuous.

Sorbus aria 'Lutescens'

S–M **AGM 1969**

Only in spring is this tree distinguishable from the common "Whitebeam". Then the emerging leaves are coated in a dense creamy-white tomentum which renders the tree most conspicuous at a distance. Soon after, the leaves become the normal grey-green.

Sorbus aucuparia 'Fastigiata'

S **AGM 1969**

So stiff and erect are the stout branches of this tree that it appears like a sentinel in the garden. The leaves are large and dark green in colour, among which the large sealing-wax-red berries are carried in large, dense bunches. It may be trained to a clear stem, or left with branches to the base. Either way, its slow growth and columnar habit qualify it for a place even in the smallest gardens. Its name is the latest in a long line and it boasts as many aliases as a confidence trickster.

Sorbus cuspidata. The "Himalayan Whitebeam" with large handsome foliage.

Sorbus cashmiriana

S

Very different in effect from the last, this rather openly branched tree bears pinnate (ash-like) leaves and pale pink flower clusters in May. These are replaced by comparatively large, glistening-white, marble-like berries which hang in loose clusters from the branches. Like most white- or yellow-berried trees this is spared the attentions of birds who seem averse to eating its berries which, as a result, remain on the branches until the leaves have fallen in late autumn. As the name implies, it is a native of Kashmir.

Sorbus cuspidata

M

The "Himalayan Whitebeam" presents a distinct erect habit as a young tree, broadening in maturity. It is mainly notable for its large, bold, often rounded leaves up to 25 cm long. These are covered in a white down when emerging, becoming greyish green above, silver-white beneath later. The creamy-white flower-clusters in May are followed, in autumn, by globular or pear-shaped brown and green berries resembling small russet "crabs". This handsome tree is a native of the Himalayas and is quite hardy and vigorous in the British Isles, happy on most soils.

Sorbus aucuparia

S–M   **AGM 1969**

The "Mountain Ash" or "Rowan" is one of the most ornamental of our native trees. The leaves are divided into numerous sharply toothed leaflets and, in late May or early June, are joined by flattened heads of creamy-white flowers. It is usually the first of the *Sorbus* to ripen its berries when, in late August or September, they turn a bright orange-red, the heavy bunches filling the branches, lighting the early autumn days until, inevitably, the black-birds take their toll. Although common and easy to grow this is one of the most reliable of small trees and is adaptable to almost any soil and situation, although on shallow chalk soils it is shorter-lived than *S. aria*. It is distributed in the wild throughout Europe and has given rise to many different forms, most of which bear similar berries. Seedlings are used as stocks for grafting the better clones of this and related species.

Sorbus aucuparia 'Beissneri'

S   **AGM 1969**

A superb tree when seen at its best. The bark of both the trunk and the erect branches is a warm coppery orange in colour which glows when wet and develops a thin whitish bloom on drying. This effect is best developed on trees growing in the drier eastern regions of the British Isles. Like several other coloured-bark trees, specimens growing in moister western areas often have the ornamental effect diminished by the tendency for algae or lichen to form on the bark. Even without the coloured bark, this tree is worth growing for its attractive leaves, which are yellow-green, especially when young, carried on red petioles, and have the leaflets deeply cut or divided to create a fern-like effect.

Sorbus hupehensis

S   **AGM 1969**

A distinct species recognisable, even from a distance, by the blue-green colour of its bold, deeply divided leaves. It is a strong-growing tree with purplish-brown branches, ascending on a young specimen. The berries in autumn are white or pink tinged and borne in loose drooping clusters lasting well into winter. A tree so laden is a welcome spectacle at Christmas time. It is a native of western China.

Sorbus aria 'Lutescens'. *Spring foliage of creamy-white.*

Sorbus aria 'Decaisneana'.*One of the best forms of the 'Whitebeam'.*

Sorbus aucuparia. A popular and reliable ornamental tree.

Sorbus aucuparia 'Fastigiata'. *A 20 year old tree grown on a clear stem.*

Sorbus hupehensis. One of the most reliable white fruited species.

Sorbus scalaris. One of the best for autumn leaves and fruit

Sorbus x kewensis. One of the heaviest fruiters.

Sorbus cashmiriana. Fruits like white marbles.

Sorbus 'Joseph Rock'. *The yellow
fruits remain well into winter, untouched by birds.*

Sorbus hybrida 'Gibbsii'.
Hardy and tolerant of most situations.

130

Sorbus hybrida 'Gibbsii'

S–M

A dense, round-headed tree with broad leaves deeply lobed at the base, dark green above and grey-felted below. The bright-red berries are produced in large bunches in autumn, standing out from the dark foliage. This is a really tough and adaptable tree for all situations.

Sorbus meliosmifolia

S

One of the many *Sorbus* from western China, this uncommon but highly ornamental tree is notable for its compact head of upright branches and its strongly and conspicuously veined, oval leaves. The clusters of white flowers appear with the young leaves in April and are later replaced by small brown berries which hang in bunches from the branches and persist until long after leaf fall.

Sorbus 'Joseph Rock'

S   **AGM 1969**

Commemorating a famous American plant collector and explorer in north-western China, this superb tree richly deserves the praise it has received and the popularity it enjoys. As with most other *Sorbus* of this group, young trees possess upswept branches forming a compact head. The deeply divided leaves are made up of numerous toothed leaflets which turn from a bright summer green to a fiery combination of orange, red, copper and purple in autumn. At the same time, the clusters of berries deepen from creamy-yellow to amber-yellow glistening amid the rosetted foliage. These remain untouched by the birds and hang from the branches until woll after the leaves have fallen.

Sorbus × kewensis

S   **AGM 1969**

Only recently has this splendid tree been given a name of its own, having for some time masqueraded under the name of *S. pohuashanensis*, of which with *S. aucuparia* it is a hybrid. It is, perhaps, the heaviest-cropping of all the mountain ashes. the branches bending under the weight of its large dense bunches of orange-red berries. Like its *aucuparia* parent its berries colour early, in September, and there is no greater autumn spectacle than a mature tree in full berry, before the birds have gone to work. As the name suggests, this tree originated in Kew Gardens.

Sorbus intermedia

S–M

The "Swedish Whitebeam" is a most adaptable tree, particularly suitable for town and city gardens where its dense, normally rounded crown is conspicuous from afar. The leaves are strongly toothed and shallowly lobed, being dark glossy green above and grey-felted below. The orange-red berries in autumn occur in bunches along the branches. It is native to north-western Europe.

Sorbus meliosmifolia.
Brown fruits and handsomely ribbed leaves.

Sorbus alnifolia. Neat in habit and colouring well in autumn.

Sorbus vilmorinii. Delicate frond-like leaves and graceful habit.

Sorbus scalaris

S **AGM 1969**

If one has space in the garden for a small but widespreading *Sorbus* of handsome and elegant appearance then this is probably the best. Its long branches arch outwards, eventually curving gently towards the ground. The leaves, which are glossy green and divided into numerous narrow leaflets, are gathered into delightful rosette-like clusters all along the boughs. Amid the leaves appear large, flattened, white flowerheads in spring, to be replaced by equally large clusters of small, late-ripening bright-red berries. The berries are generally ripening when the leaves are donning their autumn hues of red and purple. A native of western China, this is altogether a first-class all-round tree for any garden, space permitting.

Sorbus × thuringiaca 'Fastigiata'

S

In effect, the crown of this tree is more lozenge-shaped or lollipop-shaped than conical. The branches are stiffly ascending, and so closely packed that the head is dense and impenetrable. The leaves are divided to the midrib at the base and shallowly lobed elsewhere, whilst the clusters of white flowers in spring are replaced in autumn by bunches of glossy red berries. A hybrid between the "Whitebeam" (*S. aria*) and the "Rowan" (*S. aucuparia*), this easily recognisable tree possesses all the qualities of its parents, being very hardy and adaptable, particularly suitable for town and city gardens and those where space is restricted.

Sorbus vilmorinii

VS–S **AGM 1953**

A charming tree of graceful habit, highly suitable for the small garden. The slender arching branches bear clusters of small fern-like leaves, each made up of numerous, small, prettily toothed leaflets. These turn to shades of purple and red in autumn. The drooping clusters of small, rounded berries in autumn are glossy red at first, slowly changing to pink and finally white with a pink flush. They are long-lasting and decorate the naked branches after leaf fall. This is yet another desirable native of western China.

Sorbus x kewensis.
Perhaps the most reliable and satisfactory Sorbus for fruits.

STEWARTIA

A small genus of deciduous trees and shrubs notable for late summer flowering, autumn colour and ornamental bark. None are very large and all appreciate a moist but well-drained, lime-free soil and a sheltered site. They resent disturbance and are best planted small in a position where their shallow root system is shaded from the direct rays of the summer sun.

Stewartia koreana

S–M

A beautiful Korean tree of elegant growth, often conical when young. The slender-pointed leaves often give warm orange-brown or orange-red tints in autumn, while the white flowers with silky-backed spreading petals and a central tuft of stamens occur singly in the leaf axils at intervals along the branches, opening in continual succession from July into August. The bark, especially on older trees, is attractively flaking, creating a striking effect.

Stewartia pseudocamellia. A young specimen in autumn.

Stewartia pseudocamellia.
Handsome patchwork bark of an old tree.

Stewartia koreana. A young well shaped tree in autumn.

Stewartia pseudocamellia

S–M

This attractive long-flowering Japanese tree is free-growing when once established. The slender spreading or arching branches each carry numerous cup-shaped, yellow-anthered, white flowers which rapidly open and fall to be replaced by others over several weeks. Thus, throughout July and August this tree is never out of bloom. In a good autumn the leaves turn to shades of yellow, red or purple, finally succumbing to the cold fingers of winter, when, leafless and alone, a large specimen shows off its flaking bark for all to see.

STYRAX

A large genus of deciduous trees and shrubs grown mainly for their flowers and often attractive foliage. Like the "Stewartias" they thrive best in a moist but well-drained lime-free loam, in sun or semi-shade. They also resent disturbance when once established and are best planted when small, straight into their permanent position, which should be carefully prepared beforehand.

Styrax japonica. Showers of white "stars" beneath the leaves.

Styrax obassia. A young specimen displaying its handsome large leaves.

Styrax japonica

S   **AGM 1969**

To see a large flowering specimen of this beautiful tree is a most satisfying experience. Its slender fan-like branches are widespreading and are piled layer upon layer to form a dense mound. The small, white, star-like flowers have a central yellow cluster of stamens and appear, often in prodigious numbers, along the slender branchlets in June. Because they are pendulous, the flowers tend to be obscured by the dense but elegant foliage and the branches therefore need to be lifted or viewed from below in order to fully appreciate the display. In order to facilitate viewing it is sometimes planted on a convenient bank. It is a native of Japan and Korea.

Styrax obassia

S

Very different in appearance from *S. japonica*, this choice Japanese species develops a conical or rounded head of branches, with large, handsome, rounded leaves which are softly felted beneath. The bark of the previous year's shoots is chestnut-brown in colour, curling and flaking in a pleasing manner. In June the fragrant, white, bell-shaped flowers appear in long, lax racemes from the tips of the branches, but not on small young trees. In order to grow this tree well it is important to give it a good start, adding to the planting hole a nice mixture of peat and leaf mould. It also appreciates the company and shelter of other trees or large shrubs.

TILIA

The "Limes" or "Lindens" are a large genus of hardy deciduous trees occurring in the wild throughout the northern temperate regions. None are grown for their flowers which, though produced in abundance, are small and greenish yellow in colour. Several have attractive leaves, and the majority make stately specimens ideal for large gardens and parks. They are easily grown on almost all soils and are tolerant of atmospheric pollution as well as hard pruning. They may be recognised in summer by their alternately arranged heart-shaped leaves, and in winter by their zig-zag twigs.

Tilia cordata

M–L

The "Small-leaved Lime" is one of our two native species, the other being *T. platyphyllos*. It develops a handsome rounded head of branches, with small, neatly heart-shaped, rather leathery leaves of a glossy dark green above. The tiny ivory-coloured flowers in July are sweetly scented. It occurs in the wild throughout Europe.

Tilia × euchlora

M   **AGM 1969**

An elegant tree when young, becoming rather dense and twiggy, with pendulous lower branches, when older. The comparatively large, handsome leaves are rounded and of a bright glossy green above. This tree is said to be a hybrid between the "Small-leaved Lime" (*T. cordata*) and the uncommon *T. dasystyla*. It is especially noted for its healthy appearance and does not suffer from the sticky attentions of aphids in the same way as does the "Common Lime" (*T. × europaea*).

Tilia × europaea

L

Although the "Common Lime" has been extensively planted, particularly as an avenue tree, in the past, its dense and unsightly suckering habit has caused it to be relegated in favour of more desirable limes. The following cultivar, however, is worth growing for its colourful leaves.

Tilia × europaea 'Wratislaviensis'

L

An uncommon and unusual form of the "Common Lime" in which the leaves are a bright golden yellow when young, becoming green as they mature. This is a most attractive large tree in the same mould as the "Golden Poplar" (*Populus* 'Serotina Aurea').

Tilia x europaea 'Wratislaviensis'. *Golden young leaves.*

Tilia mongolica

S

The "Mongolian Lime" is one of the few species suitable for small gardens. It develops a neat, compact, rounded head of branches and is easily recognised by its small leaves which are sharply 3-lobed (at least on young trees) and strongly toothed. In fact, they resemble more those of certain thorns (*Crataegus*) and would puzzle all bar the experts on first being seen. They are a glossy green during summer, turning butter-yellow in autumn. A native of Mongolia and northern China.

Tilia mongolica. A little known lime with sharply cut leaves.

Tilia petiolaris

L   **AGM 1969**

Along with *Salix* × *chrysocoma*, the "Weeping Silver Lime" is perhaps the most spectacular of large weeping trees. The long downward-sweeping branches build up a high rounded or mounded crown thickly clothed with large rounded leaves. These are dark green above and white-felted beneath, rustling and turning in the wind in a most pleasing and attractive manner. The tiny flowers, though sweetly fragrant, are narcotic to bees. It is of unknown, possibly hybrid, origin.

Tilia platyphyllos

L

This is a large vigorous tree in the same way as *T.* × *europaea*. It differs from the "Common Lime", however, in its downy young twigs and leaves and in its relatively clean, non-suckering habit. It is found in the wild through central and southern Europe, including the British Isles and is commonly represented in cultivation by the cultivar 'Rubra'.

Tilia platyphyllos 'Laciniata'

S–M

A most effective tree of dense habit with leaves which are deeply and variously cut and toothed, often with tail-like points. It is an excellent tree to plant where the type would be too large.

Tilia tomentosa. A 18 year old tree just developing its erect-branched habit.

Tilia x euchlora.
Glossy green leaves are a feature.

Tilia platyphyllos 'Rubra'

L

The "Reg-twigged Lime" is very popular as a street tree particularly in industrial areas. In habit it is more compact and erect than the type and the bright reddish young twigs are conspicuous during winter.

Tilia tomentosa

L

Conical as a young tree, the strongly ascending branches of the "Silver Lime" gradually open up at the tips with age to present one of the most stately of all trees. The large rounded leaves are dark green above, white-felted beneath and are very effective when ruffled by a breeze. It is a native of south-eastern and east central Europe and is commonly planted as a park tree in many countries.

Tilia platyphyllos 'Lacinata'. *An attractive cut-leaved lime of compact habit.*

ULMUS

Some of the stateliest of deciduous trees are found among the "Elms". They are hardy, fast-growing trees adaptable to most soils and situations, withstanding strong winds and atmospheric pollution equally well. Their flowers are rather small and of no great ornamental merit, appearing, in most species, before the leaves in early spring. The leaves are usually peculiarly uneven at the base and turn a clear yellow in autumn. Although, of late, the elms have suffered terribly from the effects of the Dutch Elm Disease there is reason to believe that this catastrophe (and such it surely is) will gradually be overcome and elms will once more figure in our landscapes.

Ulmus angustifolia cornubiensis

L

The "Cornish Elm" has suffered from a surfeit of names in the past and has the added humiliation of being commonly confused with the "Jersey Elm" ($U. \times sarniensis$). It develops a broadly conical head of ascending branches, becoming looser and more open topped with age. It occurs as a native in Devon and Cornwall and in Brittany in France, being occasionally planted elsewhere. Like most elms it is excellent for coastal gardens where it cheerfully withstands cold and blast.

Ulmus glabra

L

One of our commonest and most satisfying native trees, the "Wych Elm" or "Scotch Elm" forms an imposing mound of massive arching branches becoming pendulous at their extremities. Its leaves are characteristically broad and rough to the touch above, almost stalkless and turning yellow in autumn. It is one of the best of all trees for maritime exposure and cold exposed inland areas. It occurs in the wild throughout Europe and into northern and western Asia.

Ulmus glabra 'Camperdownii'. *The distinctive 'mushroom' habit of the "Camperdown Elm."*

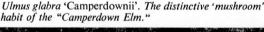

Ulmus glabra
'Camperdownii'

S

The "Camperdown Elm" is possibly even more common in gardens than the "Weeping Ash" (*Fraxinus excelsior* 'Pendula'). It is certainly more suitable in size for smaller gardens, forming a small mushroom-headed tree with densely packed branches snaking to the ground, clothed with large deep-green leaves. It is an excellent tree for lawns and grassy places.

Ulmus glabra
'Exoniensis'

L

As a young tree, this is characterised by its narrow habit and erect branches. Gradually, however, it broadens with age. The leaves are tightly clustered up the stems, adding to the unusual effect. Despite its habit when young it is not really a tree for small gardens.

Ulmus glabra
'Pendula'

S

The "Weeping Wych Elm" is a popular tree in large gardens and parks where its shade in summer is much appreciated. It is a taller and broader tree than the "Camperdown Elm", its widespreading branches arching gradually towards the ground, not steeply falling as in the other.

Ulmus × hollandica
'Dampieri'

M

Similar in effect to *U. glabra* 'Exoniensis', this makes a more compact conical tree, neater and more pleasing in appearance.

Ulmus × hollandica
'Wredei'

M

Arising as a branch sport of 'Dampieri', this colourful tree is of similar compact conical habit. The broad, crowded leaves, however, are golden yellow throughout summer.

Ulmus hollandica 'Wredei'. *A young specimen showing typical erect habit.*

Ulmus pumila arborea

S

An uncommon but easily grown, elegant elm, suitable for small gardens. The small neat leaves are arranged in opposite rows along the branchlets, which are themselves similarly arranged, giving the whole branch a fan-like appearance. It is a native of western Siberia and Turkestan.

Ulmus procera.
The splendour of an 'English Elm' in autumn.

Ulmus x sarniensis.
A typical mature specimen in winter.

Ulmus procera

L

Few more impressive tree spectacles can be gazed upon than a tall stately "English Elm", especially when clothed in its autumn gold. As a wild tree it is only found in England, where it has been, and I feel sure, will always be, an inseparable part of the landscape. However devastated its ranks have been by the attacks of Dutch Elm Disease, I am confident that in time, nature will redress the balance. Important trees may be saved by chemical protection and hopefully clones will be found resistant to the disease. A single hard winter would considerably reduce the harmful bark beetle populations.

Ulmus procera 'Argentea Variegata'

L

A striking tree when well grown, the leaves streaked, splashed and speckled with creamy white and silvery grey.

Ulmus × sarniensis

L   **AGM 1969**

The "Jersey Elm" or "Wheatley Elm" is a tall tree, narrow at first, gradually broadening and conical with age, in which state it is often mistaken for the "Cornish Elm", both also having similarly small leaves. As a wild tree it occurs in Jersey and along the Channel coast of France but is widely planted elsewhere, being an excellent wind-resister. Because of its impressive shape it is often planted as a roadside or avenue tree.

Ulmus × sarniensis 'Dicksonii'

M   **AGM 1969**

"Dickson's Golden Elm" is one of the best trees of its shape and colour. Slow-growing, it is suitable for medium-sized and large gardens, its small golden-yellow leaves providing colour from spring to autumn.

Ulmus x sarniensis. Strong growing trees showing their typical conical habit.

Ulmus procera 'Argentea Variegata'.

Ulmus pumila arborea. An elegant small-leaved elm.

Ulmus x hollandica 'Dampieri'.
Branches erect forming a compact head.

ZELKOVA

Related to the "Elms", the zelkovas are a small genus of hardy, deciduous trees and occasionally shrubs. Their ornamental value rests in their attractive leafage and sometimes stately habit. They thrive best on a deep well-drained loam and are tolerant of both shade and atmospheric pollution.

Zelkova carpinifolia.
A well-shaped specimen in summer.

Zelkova carpinifolia

L

This is definitely a tree to plant for posterity, for, although its boldly toothed leaves, turning golden in autumn, are effective enough, it isn't until a tree is maturing that its full beauty is appreciated. Large specimens may be seen in several parts of the British Isles, usually in parks or on large estates, although there is a fine specimen on a street in one of the London boroughs and another in a vicarage garden in Hampshire. Slow-growing, it gradually develops its characteristic short-trunked, erect and densely branched habit to form a conical head in maturity, somewhat like a monstrous besom. The bark is grey, similar to that of a beech, on older trees flaking attractively to create a piebald effect. It is a native of the Caucasus and northern Iran, where, in the latter region, I have seen it growing with oak trees on the northern slopes of the Elburz Mountains.

Zelkova serrata

M

Quite unlike the previous species in habit, the present tree forms a rounded head of graceful widespreading branches. The bark is grey and smooth, flaking on older trees, while the slender-pointed, boldly toothed leaves turn to bronze or reddish brown in autumn. It is a native of China and Korea as well as Japan.

A short list of further reading for those interested in growing trees

Trees and Shrubs Hardy in the British Isles by W.J. Bean, 8th edition revised.
The Pruning of Trees, Shrubs and Conifers by George Brown
A Gardeners Dictionary of Plant Names by A.W. Smith, revised by W.T. Stearn.
A Field Guide to the Trees of Britain and Northern Europe by Alan Mitchell.
The Arboricultural Association publish a selection of Advisory Booklets and Leaflets which are extremely useful to anyone contemplating planting and maintaining trees.

A small selection showing the wonderful variety of leaf shapes :   (see opposite page)

1. Acer platanoides 'Crimson King' - 2. Quercus rubra - 3. Fagus sylvatica 'Asplenifolia' - 4. Quercus frainetto - 5. Magnolia grandiflora - 6. Acer davidii 'George Forrest' - 7. Quercus velutina 'Rubrifolia' - 8. Tilia x moltkei - 9. Castanea sativa - 10. Sorbus 'Mitchellii' - 11. Alnus glutinosa 'Imperialis' - 12. Quercus coccinea - 13. Magnolia grandiflora - 14. Acer rubrum - 15. Styrax obassia - 16. Acer capillipes - 17. Betula maximowicziana.

A few deeply divided leaves
1. *Rhus glabra*
2. *Rhus trichocarpa*
3. *Acer negundo*
4. *Juglans regia 'Laciniata'*
5. *Rhus glabra*
6. *Ailanthus altissima*

A small selection of deeply lobed leaves

1. *Acer platanoides 'Dissectum'*
2. *Acer cappadocicum*
3. *Acer saccharinum*
4. *Platanus x hispanica*
5. *Betula pendula 'Dalecarlica'*
6. *Tilia mongolica*
7. *Platanus orientalis*
8. *Acer macrophyllum*

Index of Lists

Five fruits of autumn :

1. *Castanea sativa* - 2. *Crataegus tanacetifolia* - 3. *Magnolia tripetala* - 4. *Acer capillipes* - 5. *Sorbus x kewensis.*

(see opposite page)

Printed in France   2nd edition revised   © ÉDITIONS FLORAISSE Antony France.
June 1980 - Legally deposed N° 48

FLOWERING TREE CALENDAR

Late spring and early summer are the peak periods for flowering trees. But whatever the time of year, there is sure to be at least one tree showing flower, even in the "bleak midwinter". Following is a calendar of trees flowering through the seasons. It must be remembered, however, that the flowering period of many trees is spread over two consecutive months, whilst others flower intermittently over several months.

DECEMBER
Prunus subhirtella 'Autumnalis'
Arbutus unedo

JANUARY
Prunus subhirtella 'Autumna...
Prunus incisa 'Praecox'

FEBRUARY
Prunus incisa 'Praec...
Prunus subhirtella '...
Salix aegyptiaca
Salix daphnoides
Alnus incana
Arbutus x andrachnoides
Populus tremula
Prunus incisa 'February Pink'

WINT...

AUTU...

SEPTEMBER
Aralia elata
Eucryphia x nymansensis 'Nymansay'
Ligustrum lucidum
Magnolia gra...
Magnolia virg...
Sophora japonic...

OCTOBER
Arbutus x andrachnoides
Arbutus unedo
Magnolia grandiflora

NOVEMBER
Arbutus x andrachnoides
Arbutus unedo
Prunus subhirtella 'Autumnalis'